WRITTEN

ADVOCACY

WRITTEN

ADVOCACY

JAMES C. MORTON
MICHAEL E. FREEMAN

Butterworths
Toronto and Vancouver

Written Advocacy
© Butterworths Canada Ltd. 2000
December 2000

The Butterworth Group of Companies

Canada:
75 Clegg Road, MARKHAM, Ontario L6G 1A1
and
1732-808 Nelson Street, Box 12148, VANCOUVER, B.C. V6Z 2H2

Australia:
Butterworths Pty Ltd., SYDNEY

Ireland:
Butterworth (Ireland) Ltd., DUBLIN

Malaysia:
Malayan Law Journal Sdn Bhd, KUALA LUMPUR

New Zealand:
Butterworths of New Zealand Ltd., WELLINGTON

Singapore:
Butterworths Asia, SINGAPORE

South Africa:
Butterworth Publishers (Pty.) Ltd., DURBAN

United Kingdom:
Butterworth & Co. (Publishers) Ltd., LONDON

United States:
LEXIS Publishing, CHARLOTTESVILLE, Virginia

Canadian Cataloguing in Publication Data

Morton, James C. (James Cooper), 1960-
    Written Advocacy

Includes index.
ISBN 0-433-43690-5

1. Legal composition. 2. Persuasion (Rhetoric). I. Freeman, Michael E.
II. Title.

KE265.M67 2000   808'.06634   C00-932813-0
KF250.M67 2000

Printed and bound in Canada.

PREFACE

Advocacy is not new. As far back as biblical times, we read about the patriarch Abraham advocating for the continued existence of Sodom before a judge of truly awesome power. Abraham's verbal technique was brilliant and almost worked,[1] but was ultimately ineffective. Modern counsel can sympathize with the situation of a good advocate stuck with a bad case, but not necessarily with Abraham's reliance on the spoken word. Today's advocacy, you see, is mostly written.

The practice of law at the start of the 21st century is quite changed from how it used to be. There is no more of what derisively used to be called "trial by ambush", and a concomitant increase in the use of factums and, more generally, written forms of communication. To take but one example, before a recent trial, one of the authors received a call from the court office requesting that, *prior to trial*, any experts' reports, case briefs and preliminary factums be delivered to the court office so that the trial judge could read them before the start of trial. Never mind the evidentiary problem inherent in the court reading, say, an expert's report prior to the expert being qualified; the trial judge felt it wise and proper to come to trial with a view of the case established by the written report. This example (which is by no means an isolated one) proves that great care must be exercised in ensuring that the client's position is advocated fully in all written documentation.

This book is intended to be an aid towards ensuring that positions are fully and properly advocated in written form.

Writing a book on a topic as broad as written advocacy is a daunting task, even when the book is as modest as this volume. Our task has been immeasurably eased by the aid, assistance and encouragement of a large number of people.

The editorial staff at Butterworths have guided us through the often difficult and frustrating task of producing a manuscript. They have cheerfully accepted our delays, hesitations and doubts and have taken a sheaf of typing and made it into an attractive text. In this regard, the authors want to thank the Butterworths staff for their able help and assistance. Aiding them, of course, in this difficult task has been our friend Rosalie Antman, who turned what was close to illegible scribbles and incomprehensible dictation into a clearly drafted and grammatically sensible text.

We hope that your indulgence in the pleasurable and instructive reading of our efforts will result in your own written advocacy bearing these same happy features.

December 2000

James C. Morton
Michael E. Freeman

---

[1] Gen. 18:25. Abraham's plea that the righteous judge act righteously ("Shall not the Judge of all the earth do right?") is heard in courtrooms around the world daily.

TABLE OF CONTENTS

Chapter 1

STYLE AND CLARITY

WHY WRITTEN ADVOCACY?

Until very recently, written advocacy played a small part in Canadian legal practice; granted, pleadings required an element of art and factums were long required at the appellate level, but until about 1985, many pleadings were little more than adaptations from form books and appeals were few. Interlocutory motions were more unusual in the past and seldom required extensive written materials. Cases were decided by oral argument.

Since the early 1980s, and even more clearly since around 1990, the "paperless" case has vanished. Cases now involve box after box of written material. To win a case, those boxes must contain written material that will convince a court.

The lawyer's weapon is language. A lawyer acts through words, and it is through words that others are persuaded or convinced. In the Canadian context, lawyers are using spoken words less frequently. The written word must assume the role of convincing, cajoling and persuading its reader that a proposition is correct or an action should be taken.

By appealing to logic or emotion, the written word can replace the speaking advocate. The nature of written advocacy is, however, very different from that of spoken advocacy. In oral submissions, the occasional (and intentional) grammatical error — say, a double negative — can be devastatingly effective; in written submissions, such an error would be jarring and false. Appeals to emotion in written materials must be subtle. Choice of words is key; words that have emotional connotations can be used to create a mood. Similarly, word order and tense impact on how information is perceived. Regardless, the reader must not be made aware of any artifice in the choice of language. The moment that you realize that you are looking through rose-coloured glasses, the effect is mostly lost; once the reader perceives artifice, all persuasion vanishes.

WHO IS THE READER AND HOW WILL HE OR SHE REACT?

Writing must adapt to and anticipate its reader. Obviously, the reader's sophistication needs to be accounted for, but the reader's inherent or institutional bias towards the situation must also considered. A judge will look at the situation differently than a business person, a party or a witness. Lawyers working in a large multi-jurisdictional firm doing tax work view cases differently than sole practitioners of family law.

Judges are the most important readers of legal writing, and they look at cases from an institutional standpoint of justice and fairness. Judges want matters to be concluded quickly and with a minimum of judicial interference. This is a very different perspective from that held by many members of the legal community and their clients. Judges will be inclined to rule in a fashion that will resolve a dispute — unless clearly necessary, a judge will avoid rulings that expand litigation or lengthen proceedings. Remember: Each reader must be moved to act as counsel wants. This means speaking to the reader and addressing his or her concerns.

Legal writing is not intended to be uplifting, to evoke emotional response, or to make the reader laugh. Remember: *each reader must be moved to act as counsel wants.* Even in a controversy — where litigation against the reader is imminent — good counsel is trying to get the reader to do something. Why write if not to get the reader to do something your way?

Legal writing requires consideration for the level of the reader. The reader should never be insulted or patronized; abuse may serve as a catharsis for the writer but it is poor advocacy and wasted effort. A good rule of thumb is to ask: If I received this letter, claim, or whatever, how would I react? Does that reaction help or hurt your client's position? If it does not help your case, rewrite until you can move the reader to act the way you want.

Contradictory information or unhelpful information can be used to move a reader. An argument is often more convincing if it freely admits strong counter arguments or bad facts. Candor leads trust to a document. By delivering unhelpful information fairly, but in such a way as to lead to a resounding counterargument, your initial argument is strengthened enormously. Judges, especially, are impressed with an even-handed presentation of facts and arguments.

STYLE AND CLARITY

It is sometimes said that the shoemaker's children are the ones most likely to go barefoot. Certainly there is something to be said for the concept that familiarity breeds contempt. But as a lawyer, it is important to remember that clients and non-lawyers seldom see anything legal as trivial. People see lawyers for matters they perceive as being of grave importance. Therefore, in the legal context it is safe to assume a certain seriousness of tone. That said, in dealing with judges and other lawyers it is often appropriate to be somewhat more light-hearted. As noted before, considering the reader and appreciating his or her preconceptions and concerns is likely sufficient to avoid stylistic problems. Jokes are not appropriate in factums; holiday greetings in letters to counsel are appropriate.

Everything you write ought to have a purpose; this means clarity is essential. Regardless of what you want to say, unless the reader can understand what you mean, your language will accomplish nothing. Before you begin to write, you must know what you are trying to say. Joseph Williams notes:[1]

> Writing can be a fruitfully circular process: we have to understand what we want to say in order to write clearly and concisely. And if we can't write what we mean clearly and concisely enough or, when necessary, clearly though complexly enough, we won't be able to understand exactly what we should be saying. If we can write and then quickly rewrite syntactical confusion into clear prose, we'll understand our ideas better. And when we understand our ideas better, we the will write more clearly, and if we write more clearly, we'll will understand even better.

Anything that can be clearly thought can be clearly written. Clearly written materials are convincing — a muddle is not.

TIPS ON CLARITY AND COHERENCE

For clear and coherent writing:

1. Make your verbs, adverbs and adjectives specific.

   Don't write:

   The plan of the litigation department is the improvement of efficiency.

   Write:

   The litigation department plans to improve efficiency.

2. Make your nouns the subjects of the verb's actions.

   Don't write:

   The ruling on the part of the board in regard to jurisdiction must be made for there to be adequate Ministry preparation.

   Write:

   If the Ministry is to prepare adequately, the board must rule on jurisdiction.

3. Cut out unnecessary language. Legal writing is full of words like "general", "in most cases", "often" and the like — these words can be cut out. Similarly, when a single word will do, cut out a phrase.

---

[1]   Joseph Williams, *Style* (Glensville: Scott, Foresman & Co., 1989), p. 5.

4. Shorten your sentences. Complex ideas do not require complex sentences. Review any sentence that is more than three lines long to see if it can broken into smaller sentences. An important idea can be lost to the reader if it is crowded together with other, less important ideas.

Joseph Williams summarized clear writing as follows:[2]

When we link the simple point that sentences are stories about characters who act to the way we use the grammar of the sentence to describe those characters and their actions, we get a principal of style more powerful than any other. It is a principle that explains how turgid prose really differs from clear prose; but more important, it also tells us how to revise one into the other. Here is the principle. It has two parts: one, in the subjects of your sentences, name your cast of characters; two, in the verbs of your sentences, name the crucial actions which involve those characters.

Good legal writing is a lifelong quest. Luckily for you, you'll get a lot of opportunity to practise.

---

[2]   Joseph Williams, *Style* (Glensville: Scott, Foresman & Co., 1989), p. 5.

Chapter 2

GRAMMAR

INTRODUCTION

One of the most important rules of written advocacy is also one of the most obvious: avoid annoying the reader. Challenging the reader is fine, but having the reader focus on the form of the text rather than its message is not.

In the legal profession, writing style is an issue before the first letter is on the paper. Ask the public what comes to mind when they think of lawyers and their list of stereotypes will include communication in "legalese". Groucho Marx got a lot of mileage from his dictation of a mock legal letter, which began: "Gentlemen, question mark, re: yours of the 15th, quote unquote in quotes…we require an *ipso facto* which is non-negligible…".

Actually, good legal writing is nothing more or less than good writing, period. If at all possible, the text itself is invisible — in other words, any non-standard grammar should be avoided. As Constance Rooke points out:[1]

> To dangle one's participles in public is to invite at least momentary disap-
> proval and distrust — for the Emperor (and all his lieutenants) really
> should be clothed. Lawyers and judges of my acquaintance seem particu-
> larly given to secret criticism of one another's prose. And, of course, clients
> want to know that they can rely upon their lawyers and so are likely to
> scrutinize very carefully whatever evidence of expertise they may possess
> — your letters being the most obvious example.

This chapter focuses on a number of areas to watch, as well as some common words and phrases that are prone to give trouble from time to time.

---

[1] Constance Rooke, *A Grammar Booklet for Lawyers* (Toronto: Law Society of Upper Canada, 1991), p. 2.

VERB FORMS

Stating the Obvious: The form of a verb must agree with both the tense and the person of the verb's subject. The verb must also agree in number with its subject.

Verb problems can arise within a lengthy and complex sentence. The statement "He have gone away" is obviously wrong. But the same error in the following sentence is not so clear:

He, having finished packing his equipment and ensuring its safe storage, have gone away.

Use your eyes and (mental) ears when you're parsing verbs. When in doubt, isolate the verb and its subject and put them together in a short sentence — any errors will immediately leap out.

PERSONAL PRONOUNS

Personal pronouns can cause difficulties in compound constructions.[2] There's nothing wrong with saying "Mary went away with her", but the sentence "Mary and her went away" is grammatically wrong. It is not, however, as obviously wrong as "Her went away", and that's the way you can avoid making this common mistake: Mentally isolate the personal pronoun, putting it alone with the verb. If it works alone, it will work in a group.

SPELING ERRURS

Spelling errors in legal writing have the same effect as meeting a client and sporting a mustard stain on your chin. The incongruity jumps out at the reader and immediately robs the text of its persuasive authority. In fact, spelling mistakes create the instant impression of ignorance and carelessness. Don't forget: You never get a second chance to make a first impression.

A few hints on spelling: Non-standard spelling should be avoided. Fortunately, virtually all word processing packages now have spell-checking features which can pick up most common spelling errors. Unfortunately, spell-checking features will not highlight a word that is properly spelled but not the one you had in mind. Think of the potential for disaster when you write "illicit" instead of "elicit", or when you leave the "t" out of "Morton".

The only cure for spelling errors is the traditional one: you must carefully proofread your documents. When you come to a word that you

---

[2]   For example, "she and Bob" or "him and Mary".

think may be wrongly spelled, take the time to look it up and correct it. If you have the available human resources, ask someone else to proofread your documents — others will read what you wrote, rather than what you *thought* you wrote. If no outside proofreader is on hand, try putting aside your document for a day and then proofread it yourself. The fresh perspective will allow you to pick up many errors you might well have missed the day before.

SENTENCE FRAGMENTS

A sentence fragment is a non-sentence structured to look like a sentence.[3] For example, "Someone with experience." is a sentence fragment. In general, sentence fragments should be avoided. They lack sense and are choppy to read. It is usually best to add the sentence fragment to a neighbouring sentence. Here's an example:

The firm needed another associate. Preferably someone with a client base.

is better written

The firm needed another associate, preferably someone with a client base.

You can also expand a sentence fragment into a full sentence of its own:

The firm needed another associate. The preferred candidate would be someone with a client base.

Sentence fragments don't always have to be avoided. Legal writing, after all, is a form of persuasive expression. Used sparingly, the sentence fragment can give emphasis to a document, especially if it answers a stated question:

What type of sentence is required for a breach of trust conviction? Jail, and a lengthy term at that.

COMMA SPLICES

As a general rule, it is improper to link two main clauses together. For example, it sounds awkward to say:

The case was unanswerable, the defendant pleaded guilty.

A spliced sentence is hard to read and stands out. Correcting a common splice is usually easy: Replace the comma with a semicolon:

The case was unanswerable; the defendant pleaded guilty.

---

[3] It starts with a capital letter and ends with a period.

Another way to fix a comma splice is to turn a spliced sentence into two sentences, or to make one of the clauses subordinate to the other. Often, revising a spliced sentence turns awkward into sensible:

The case was unanswerable, the defendant pleaded guilty.

becomes

The case was unanswerable. The defendant pleaded guilty.

or

The case was unanswerable, so the defendant pleaded guilty.

DOUBLE NEGATIVES

Double negatives often occur in spoken language, and they can be an effective way of being emphatic — "Old Man River, he must know somethin', but he don't say nothin'". As long as you use double negatives intentionally, they can make your speech homey and personal.

Double negatives seldom pose problems in written language because they don't occur often. Written double negatives can confuse the reader as to the author's meaning — is the usage for emphasis or to actually negate the negative? Is the sentence "He has not got no money" a strong way of saying "He has no money", or does it mean "He is not impecunious"? Double negatives can easily creep into writing, especially in lengthy sentences written in the passive voice.

Remember: double negatives usually work best in an informal setting, where the listener can pick up contextual clues from the speaker's voice. When writing in a legal context, double negatives should be used sparingly and judiciously.

MISPLACED MODIFIERS

Did you ever hear about the beautiful professor's daughter?

Misplacing a modifier is a time-honoured technique for setting up sentences that do not mean what you want them to mean. A good general rule is to keep modifiers and the words they modify as close as possible. For example, notice how changing the position of a single word can change the meaning of a sentence:

Only John does cases in Newmarket.

or

John does only cases in Newmarket.

or

John does cases only in Newmarket.

As you can see, the meanings of identical words can vary greatly, just by the order in which they're written. Here are those sentences "in translation":

Only John does cases in Newmarket.

means

No one else does cases in Newmarket.

John does only cases in Newmarket.

means

John does nothing other than cases in Newmarket.

John does cases only in Newmarket.

means

John does cases in no jurisdiction other than Newmarket.

Keeping sentences straight is essential if you are to be understood and persuasive. This means that modifiers should never be placed between two potential "modifiees". Otherwise, you might end up with the beautiful professor's daughter, and leave your reader wondering just who is beautiful — is it the professor or the daughter? Consider the following:

The parties agreed during the recess to go to mediation.

This could mean either of two things:

During the recess, the parties agreed to go to mediation.

or

The parties agreed to go to mediation during the recess.

Ambiguity is the enemy of clarity, and clarity is what legal writing is all about. Remain on guard!

CAPITALIZATION

Capitalization is a fairly mechanical process because many of its rules are universal and standard. We all know that the first word in each sentence ought to be capitalized. In a legal context, there is a list of specific words that are always capitalized. (The list appears at the end of this section.)

One issue that occasionally arises is the capitalization of pronouns referring to a judge or judicial officer. Normally such pronouns would not be capitalized. For example,

Mr. McNeely is a prominent lawyer who practises criminal law.

It is unnecessary to capitalize "lawyer", "criminal", or "law".

A judge or judicial officer will have her or his mode of address capitalized, but not the relevant pronoun. For example,

> *Justice Collins is a prominent judge in Truro. His Honour sits in criminal court, where he has been assigned for the past 20 years.*

Notice that the title "His Honour" is capitalized. The pronoun "he" alone is not. (In fact, capitalizing pronouns other than "I" in the middle of sentences is generally reserved only for God.)

Like most matters in today's legal writing, usage of capitals is not mandatory, but a matter of style. Still, you might wish to observe convention for this list:

WORDS THAT MUST OR OUGHT TO BE CAPITALIZED

Proper names of persons and things
Geographical names
Names of peoples
Names of languages
Days of the week, months and holidays
Companies, government agencies and other organizations
Historical events, documents, periods and movements
Religions, gods, holy books, holy days
Acronyms
Titles that precede the name of the title holder
Trademarks
Titles and subtitles of books, journals and legislation
Words derived from proper nouns

PROBLEMATIC WORDS AND PHRASES

The English language is filled with pairs of words that are almost identical. Some of these pairs mean almost the same thing. In the realm of written advocacy, however, almost the same thing is not good enough.

Here are some word pairs that show up repeatedly:

A while and *awhile*. *Awhile* is an adverb meaning "for a time". *A while*, by contrast, is a noun phrase denoting a period of time.

> *She had to think for a while before deciding to sue.*

> *The mediator spoke awhile at the start of the process.*

Adverse and *averse*. *Adverse* means "unfavourable" or "opposed to". *Averse* means "to have a distaste for".

> *The parties were adverse in interest.*

> *They are averse to settling without an apology letter.*

Affect and *effect*. Used as a verb, *affect* means to influence or to display a character ostentatiously or falsely.

Used as a verb, *effect* means "to bring about".

Commencing litigation will affect the way the parties deal with each other.

Duty counsel affected the tone of someone who cared.

Commencing litigation will effect an immediate termination of the business relations between the parties.

Affect is not used as a noun, except as a specialized psychological term. Used as a noun, *effect* means "result".

Litigation will affect business greatly.

The effect of litigation is seldom conducive to business relations.

Council, counsel and *consul*. This is a dangerous trio that confuses many writers. A *council* is a board or tribunal. A *consul* is an emissary to a foreign country. *Counsel* can be used as either a noun or a verb. As a noun, it can mean a lawyer or the advice a lawyer gives. As a verb, to *counsel* someone is to give advice.

The City Council will meet Thursday.

The French consul was warmly received by the audience.

Counsel are to meet with prisoners only between lunch and dinner.

I will counsel the prisoner on her rights.

Eminent and *imminent*. *Eminent* means "famous" or "prominent", while *imminent* means "about to take place", usually with an implicit element of danger.

Safia Muhammed, Q.C., is an eminent lawyer.

Unless the dispute is resolved, litigation is imminent.

Formally and *formerly*. *Formally* is "in a formal fashion", while *formerly* means "previously".

We write to propose, formally, a settlement of this action.

Formerly we were counsel to the plaintiff.

Ingenious and *ingenuous*. *Ingenious* means "brilliant" or "very clever", while *ingenuous* means "lacking subtlety" or "having a childlike innocence".

The expert witness was ingenious and made a good impression on the jury.

The plaintiff's lawyer presented an ingenuous argument for punitive damages; the judge had to conceal her laughter.

Its and *it's*. Here's a classic pair. *Its* means "belonging to it". *It's* is the contraction of "it is".

The plaintiff corporation has moved and its new offices are much larger than its old offices.

It's a pity we have to litigate this matter without a retainer.

Liable and *libel*. *Liable* means "responsible" (usually for payment of damages). *Libel* is written defamation.

The defendant is liable for breach of contract.

The journalist's statements constitute libel.

(Equestrian fans will also add former Canadian Olympian Terry *Leibel*.)

Principal and *principle*. *Principle* is a noun which describes a moral rule or general truth. *Principal* can be a noun or an adjective which means, among other things, "a person in charge"; "capital lent or borrowed"; "most important"; "chief" or "main".

It is best to act on the principle that the party opposite is not forthright.

The bank's principal source of revenue is from lending.

Stationary and *stationery*. *Stationary* means "not moving", while *stationery* refers to writing materials, such as letterhead and envelopes.

Counsel should remain stationary while addressing a jury.

Please order more letterhead and office stationery.

Whose and *who's*. *Whose* indicates possession. *Who's* is a contraction of "who is".

The company, whose trademark is a green tree, is in the environmental business.

Knock, knock; who's there?

Your, *you're*, and *yore*. *Your* means "belonging to you", while *you're* is the contraction of "you are". *Yore* is an archaic way of saying "long ago", and should not be used in legal writing.

Your documents have been filed.

You're very late for court.

A dollar bought a good meal in days of yore.

OTHER EASILY CONFUSED WORD PAIRS

There are other pairs of words which don't sound alike, but are often confused for one another. Consider these examples:

Who and *whom*. The distinction between these words is difficult and, some would argue, archaic. These days, you can get away with using *who* at all times. If you're a stickler, remember that *who* and *whom* both mean "which specific person", but *whom* is usually preceded by "to".

Who spilled coffee on my Criminal Code?

To whom were these remarks addressed?

Advised and *informed*. This is another word pair whose distinctiveness has become blurred. Traditionally, to be *advised* suggests receiving communication which includes some element of counsel. To be *informed*, on the other hand, suggests communication without comment. *Informed* is purely factual; *advised* is judgmental.

We advise against accepting the proposal because we believe you can do better.

I am informed that there will be a change of time for the start of discovery.

It is perfectly proper, however, to tell the court that "My client advises me…". There is a presumption that your clients are the ones giving you instructions; therefore, their information is elevated to the rank of advice. Try not to laugh too hard.

Anxious and *eager*. Both of these words refer to excited anticipation of an upcoming event. *Anxious*, however, also connotes the element of anxiety or nervousness, so be careful not to use it unless these emotions are also present.

The children were anxious to meet their father, who had been in jail for three years.

The lawyer was eager to receive his exorbitant retainer.

Can and *may*. *Can* refers to the ability to do something. *May* refers to having permission to do something. *Can* is also sometimes used (incorrectly) to refer to permission, but this is ungrammatical and should be avoided.

Can you have the document ready by Wednesday?

May I send the offer to settle?

Deduction and *induction*. These are two different types of reasoning. *Deduction* is drawing an inference after considering a general fact and applying it to a particular situation. *Induction*, by contrast, is an inference based on generalizing from a specific case.

The deduction was that, since all Canadians pay taxes, and since Bob was a Canadian, Bob therefore pays taxes.

Based on litigating hundreds of divorce cases, I have come to the induction that divorce is always a great emotional strain on the parties.

Imply and *infer*. *Imply* means "to express a thought indirectly", while *infer* means "to derive a conclusion from facts or premises".

The affidavit implies, but does not state directly, that the plaintiff is a liar.

We infer from your failure to respond to our recent letter that you will not consent to setting aside default.

Lay and *lie*. *Lay* means to put or set something down. *Lie* means to knowingly tell a falsehood or to rest in a horizontal position.

Please lay the documents on the boardroom table.

The defendants told lies in their statements to the police.

After losing the murder trial, the solicitor felt sick and had to lie down.

Unqualified and *disqualified*. *Unqualified* means lacking qualification. *Disqualified* means having had qualification withdrawn.

The applicant is unqualified for the secretarial position.

The articling student, having been caught cheating, is disqualified from being called to the Bar this year.

OTHER COMMON PITFALLS

Either ... or. Either and *or* are a pair of words that present the reader with a choice. Stylistically, the structure following *either* and *or* must be the same.

Either counsel can appear today or counsel can appear next Wednesday.

Neither ... nor. As with *either* and *or*, the construction following *neither* and *nor* must be the same.

The contract is satisfactory to neither the contractor nor the supplier.

Warning: It is always an error to combine *neither* with *or*!

Regardless and *irrespective*. *Regardless* and *irrespective* both mean "without regard to". The problem arises when the two words are combined to form the Frankensteinian hybrid "irregardless". To many people who earn their living by the proper use of English (like lawyers, for instance), encountering "irregardless" on paper is the equivalent of hearing nails scratching a blackboard. It is also a surefire way to acquire the label of ignoramus — so beware!

Regardless of the defendant's delaying tactics, we will set the matter down for trial this month.

The accused will receive a suspended sentence for shoplifting, irrespective of her previous convictions for the same offence.

WHY DOES IT MATTER?

Every profession or trade has its own areas of expert skill and style, something which absolutely has to be done correctly. Amateur musicians can get away with playing wrong notes, but we expect concert artists to perform without mistakes. Amateur cooks think nothing of slapping food onto their plates, but gourmet restaurant chefs make the presentation of a meal an obsessive priority. Closer to home, the average person wouldn't care if a casual conversation with someone on the street featured a couple of split infinitives or incorrect use of "who" and "whom". But when we're dealing with lawyers, we expect their grammar to be nothing short of impeccable.

Looking at it from the other angle, a lawyer who mangles the English language immediately creates a bad impression of their knowledge and competence. We expect heightened thinking processes from our barristers, so grammatical mistakes immediately start us thinking, "If this person doesn't know that 'irregardless' isn't a word, just how much law does he know?"

The correlation between bad grammar and bad lawyering is often more than just a prejudice. Consider this story:

I was once retained by a pair of teenagers who were caught up in a bitter divorce between their parents. The family had lived in Wyoming before the wife took the children and fled to her parents' home in Toronto. The husband went to court in Wyoming and obtained an *ex parte* order requiring that the children be returned from Toronto to the jurisdiction of the Wyoming court. My clients, who had been physically abused by their father, were adamant about not wishing to return.

I was certain that the husband had neglected to tell the Wyoming court that he beat his children, and I was equally certain that the judge would have ruled differently had she known these facts. I therefore wrote a letter to the judge (with a copy to the husband's lawyer) identifying myself as counsel for the children. I explained that my clients did not wish to return to Wyoming and asked the judge to reopen the hearing. Permission was requested to submit evidence on the children's behalf because, as I explained, we took the position that the *ex parte* order had been obtained by the commission of fraud.

My letter produced a quick result. The husband's lawyer faxed me an angry letter denying the abuse charges. He then went on to write that "your claim that the court order was obtained by fraud is incredulous". *Incredulous.* As soon as I read that one word, I knew that I would not be dealing with someone overly competent. Subsequent events would prove me right.

[You see the error, of course: What the Wyoming lawyer meant to say was "your claim...is *incredible*".]

The moral of the story: Written expression is the calling card and disembodied representation of a lawyer. Make sure the image you project is flawless.

Chapter 3

CIVIL PLEADINGS

INTRODUCTION

Civil actions (including lawsuits and divorces) are begun with pleadings. If an action goes the full distance it will move through the stages of pleadings, discoveries, pre-trial motions, pre-trials and trials. The event which gets the ball rolling is the service of pleadings, namely a statement of claim, a statement of defence and, in some cases, a reply.

The word *pleadings* is archaic, part of the stultified English which used to make the law so mysterious and formal (and inaccessible to the ordinary citizen). It is, however, an accurate term: picture the plaintiff appearing before a judge and begging for justice, and you have a pretty good idea of exactly what pleadings are all about. As a modern lawyer, your job is to represent your client's interests in a busy court with too many cases on the docket, and in front of a judge who likely has not had the time to delve thoroughly into the facts of your matter. It therefore is essential that pleadings be drafted succinctly, accurately and in a very easy-to-read form. Remember: judges are not impressed with your use of legal terminology, nor will you win any "brownie points" for having sentences that run on endlessly. Which, as you will see, will bring us to Pleadings Drafting Rule #1.

THE ROLE OF PLEADINGS

Pleadings are the basis of all civil suits. What is, or is not, relevant to a case; what can, or cannot, be adduced at trial; what remedies a court can, or cannot, grant: all of these are determined by the pleadings. Even at an appeal years after the action is commenced, the scope of argument is governed by what has been pleaded. It is common for appeals to be stopped dead in their tracks by an appellant court saying, "the arguments may be all well and good but they weren't pleaded so you can't raise them here".

James Caskey, Q.C. has noted four interrelated, functions of pleadings:[1]

1. To define the questions in controversy with clarify and precision;
2. To give fair notice of the case to be met;
3. To assist the court's adjudication; and
4. To constitute a record of the issues litigated.

Tactical considerations also suggest that pleadings ought to be drafted
with care. Eminent counsel has noted:[2]

> The statements of claim and defence are the first documents to meet the
> eyes of the trial judge, and even masters or judges hearing interlocutory
> applications are affected and impressed by lucid pleadings.

By exchanging pleadings, the parties formally narrow the issues in
dispute between them so that the judge, on reading the pleadings, can
know quite specifically what is to be decided. At base, the test of a
pleading is "Can a judge, by reading the pleading, say what question
must be answered?"

FORMAL RULES

The formal requirements for pleadings are set out in rules of practice for
each relevant jurisdiction.[3] Despite surface differences, the rules of
practice generally require that all pleadings set out material facts that
disclose a reasonable cause of action or defence.[4] The basic rule of
pleading, which dates from the 1870s,[5] is set out in Ontario r. 25.06(1) as
follows:[6]

> **25.06**(1) Every pleading shall contain a concise statement of the material
> facts on which the party relies for the claim or defence, but not the evi-
> dence by which those facts are proved.

---

[1] J. Caskey, "Winning Pleadings", *Advocacy 2000* (Toronto: CBA-O, 1999), p. 2-3.
[2] Ronald Manes, *Organized Advocacy* (Toronto: Carswell, 1983), p. 6-3.
[3] See, for example, Ontario Rule 25, or Federal Rule 174.
[4] J. Caskey, "Winning Pleadings", *Advocacy 2000* (Toronto: CBA-O, 1999), p. 2.
[5] W.V. Sasso, "Advocacy Before Trial", *Insight* (Toronto: Insight, 1987), p. 1.
[6] Rules of Civil Procedure, R.R.O. 1990, Reg. 1994, as am. Compare with Federal Court
     Rules, 1998, SOR/98-106 174:
>   **174.** Every pleading shall contain a concise statement of the material facts on
>   which the party relies, but shall not include the evidence by which those facts are to
>   be proved.

This leaves a broad scope for discretion but, generally, bald assertions of law[7] or factually irrelevant allegations[8] will be struck.

PLEADING DRAFTING RULE #1

Whether you're representing the claimant (more properly known as the plaintiff) or the defendant, certain stylistic rules apply to the pleadings you draft. Here's an obvious one: Always state your case as clearly and briefly as possible.

If you are representing a plaintiff, state your case clearly in answer to the question "Why are you coming before the court in the first place?" The answer is, of course, that a law has been broken, which has caused a loss to your client, and the court has jurisdiction to remedy this breach of the law by awarding some sort of relief. Prepare yourself for Pleading Drafting Rule #2.

STATEMENT OF CLAIM

A lawsuit is begun by filing and serving a *statement of claim*. Generally, the claim will define the scope of the litigation[9] and, regardless of the particular rule of practice, contains certain specific items. Although often considered self-evident, points like what actual relief is sought and who are parties to the claim, can have a significant effect on the course of the litigation regardless of the substantive issues. All claims must contain at least the following:

1. Relief sought;
2. Parties to the claim; and
3. Substance of the claim.

The structure of these elements makes the difference between an effective claim and an ineffective claim.

PLEADING DRAFTING RULE #2

A statement of claim should outline the relief sought, the facts of the case, and the law that has been violated.

---

[7] *Genge v. Federal Business Development Bank* (1990), 85 Nfld. & P.E.I.R. 275 (Nfld. T.D.); *Allan v. New Mount Sinai Hospital* (1981), 33 O.R. (2d) 603 (C.A.).

[8] *Murphy v. Stasiuk* (1995), 44 C.P.C. (3d) 200 (Ont. Gen. Div.).

[9] *Kellogg v. Imperial* (1996), 136 D.L.R. (4th) 686 (Ont. Gen. Div.).

RELIEF SOUGHT

When drafting a claim, the effect of the claim on the defendant is worth keeping in mind. Most litigation settles, and the relief sought can be part of setting a tone that can assist in settlement. Further, if you go to trial, an excessive claim will damage your credibility. While the relief sought ought not to be minimized — claim what is sought with a proper margin for error — excessive claims should be avoided. If damages in the range of, say, $40,000 are anticipated, claiming relief of $50,000 is sensible and proper, while claiming $500,000 is not. Similarly, if the case presents the need for interim relief, claim in detail what is sensible, but no more. On this issue, detail in the injunctive relief can be very helpful in letting the defendant know just how serious the situation is. Compare the following paragraphs:

(a) *such interim, interlocutory orders restraining the defendant from competing with the plaintiff in breach of the defendant's obligations to the plaintiff as to this court seems fit and proper...*

or

(b)(i) *an order that the defendant be restrained from contacting and doing business with, directly or indirectly, any customers or former customers of the plaintiff; and*

(ii) *an order requiring the defendant to keep records of all business contacts with any customers, new or otherwise, and provide access of such records to the plaintiff; and*

(iii) *such companion orders and declarations as necessary to bring into effect the orders claimed above.*

A defendant reading the first paragraph would not likely be impressed with the seriousness of the relief sought while the second brings home the alleged breach of duty in a very clear way.

FACTS OF THE CASE

Parties to the Claim

The choice of who is to be a party is often obvious. When suing on a contract, for instance, the parties to the contract must be named. Sometimes the substantive law requires a party to be named.[10] At a minimum, all parties necessary to allow the substantive law to operate must be named.

The precise legal status and standing of a client must be determined at the very outset of proceedings. Legal concepts often elude clients and it

---

[10] As in an assignor of a contract: *Canadian Acceptance v. Southcott*, [1972] 2 O.R. 163 (Master).

is common, for example, for shareholders of private companies to say they own the company's assets, or for beneficiaries of trusts to believe they hold the trust's assets directly. Even where clients are clear on legal concepts, for example, of ownership, the distinction between corporate and personal ownership is clear, but a confusion about what corporation owns what may exist. While it is usually possible to amend pleadings to reflect the correct ownership or status, such amendments detract from the document's credibility. Ensure that you know who your client is before drafting a pleading.

The question of what other parties can, or ought, to be added should be considered carefully. For example, if a claim is made and an obvious but perhaps unnecessary party is omitted, a presumption that there was some oddity in the facts arises. For example, it is perfectly proper to make a claim in conspiracy without naming all the co-conspirators,[11] but such a claim is odd. In matters of persuasion, leaving out obvious parties weakens a claim. Similarly, adding parties against whom a case is weak does not help a claim[12] — where many doubtful parties are added, the action against the clearly liable defendants is weakened. An additional problem is that more defendants usually means more delay and, generally, a plaintiff (whether directly or by counterclaim) wants to go to trial as quickly as possible.

If sued, your client has little choice but to be a defendant, albeit perhaps also a plaintiff by counterclaim. In other situations, however, there may be a choice between being a plaintiff or defendant. It may be that the choice to be, say, a plaintiff can add credibility to an otherwise questionable defence. For a mortgagor on a defaulting mortgage (before the mortgagee moves to enforce), waiting will certainly lead to a claim. Suing first and claiming that the mortgage is invalid may give more credibility to what would otherwise be an apparently boilerplate but insubstantial defence.

Substance of the Claim

The substance of a claim depends on the facts and the substantive law. Recognizing that material facts, but only material facts, should be pleaded leads to the question of what claim is being asserted.[13] Each

---

[11] *Rose Park Wellesley Investments Ltd. v. Sewell*, [1973] 1 O.R. 102 (Master).

[12] A tactical exception to this principle exists for claims made to obfuscate the liability of the plaintiff. Such claims usually arise as claims over or counterclaims and are part of an "octopus defence" — squirt a lot of ink around and hope you can slink away in the fog. Our interest in such (abusive) claims is limited and we will not expand on it further.

[13] Certain legal matters must be raised explicitly. The matters requiring explicit pleading include:
> Judicial notice;
> Foreign law;
> Specific statutes and regulations;

claim has certain constituent elements that have to exist for the claim to succeed.[14] Those elements must be pleaded. Precedent books[15] are helpful sources for the elements of causes of action. That said, slavish adherence to a precedent book creates a formally correct, but generally unconvincing, claim. Copying a precedent will not lead to a convincing claim. Pleading the necessary elements of a cause of action is the start, not the end, of drafting.

Most claims are best told chronologically as stories. Explain how the parties come together and what happened. Excluding extraneous information and focusing the claim on the specific facts giving rise to liability is essential. That does not mean that a claim should read as a hypothetical fact scenario of disembodied beings. Tell enough about the plaintiff to make them real and personalize the plaintiff — call the plaintiff by his or her name ("Bob Clarke") and not some title ("the plaintiff" or "the lender"). Similarly, consider the legal effect of language: "Calling a person a trespasser may make him a trespasser in the eyes of a decision maker."[16] Labelling is often prescriptive and not just descriptive.

Within paragraphs of the claim, concrete language tells a far more compelling story then abstract language.[17] Hence, for a claim (as opposed to most defences), concrete language is more likely to convince a reader. Compare

> *Following the failure of the engine, as a result of the defendant's delict, the plaintiff's vehicle was unable to proceed and was impacted by a vehicle. Damage to the plaintiff's possessions and injury to the plaintiff was occasioned thereby.*

or

> *While Alice was driving on the QEW her engine blew up because the garage did not put the oil pan on properly. Alice's car came to an abrupt halt and she was hit by the car behind her on the highway. As a result, Alice broke her arm, chipped a tooth and hit her head. She has not fully recovered. Further, Alice's car was badly damaged and had to be scrapped and she lost all the cassette tapes and clothing she had in the trunk of her car.*

The first paragraph, while likely correct,[18] does not convey a sense of how awful the accident was for Alice. The second paragraph, while still

---

      Aggravation and mitigation;

      Contributory negligence; and

      Notice.

    See Ronald Manes, *Organized Advocacy*, (Toronto: Carswell, 1983), p. 6-14.

[14]   For example, duty is an element of tort — absent duty, tort cannot succeed.

[15]   J. Jacob, *Bullen & Leake & Jacob Precedents of Pleadings* (London: Sweet and Maxwell, 1990) or R.J. Rolls, *Williston & Rolls Court Forms* (Toronto: Butterworths, 1987).

[16]   Walter Probert, "Law and Persuasion" (1959), 108 U. of Penn. L.R. 35, 47. Karl Llewellyn described a case that was lost because a contract was described as being one of agency (and thus fiduciary) instead of, say, brokerage (which had no fiduciary implication): "A Lecture on Appellate Advocacy" (1962), 29 U. Chicago L. Rev. 627.

[17]   Paul Perell, "Written Advocacy", *Advocacy 2000* (Toronto: CBA-O, 1999), pp. 5, 6.

[18]   Assuming particulars of damage are pleaded elsewhere.

formal enough for a pleading, lets the reader have some feeling for what happened on a personal level. Judges are human and will react to concrete language more directly than to pleadings that sound like law school hypotheticals.

SAMPLE CLAIM #1

Obviously, each proceeding has a different claim and its form has to match the nature of the claim. That said, let's look at a sample statement of claim and see how it follows our principles.

You are acting as counsel for a family of homeowners who recently suffered property damage as the result of a home invasion. The perpetrator has been identified and your clients wish to commence an action for monetary damages.

All pleadings should be written in double-spaced numbered paragraphs for ease of reference. The first paragraph is always a statement of the relief sought. If that relief involves money, the amount should be spelled out and the categories of the relief should also be enumerated:

STATEMENT OF CLAIM

1. *The plaintiffs, Mama Bear, Papa Bear and Baby Bear (by his litigation guardian Mama Bear) claim damages from the defendant, Goldie Locks as follows:*

(a) *General damages in the amount of $5,000;*

(b) *Special damages in the amount of $3,000;*

(c) *Exemplary and punitive damages in the amount of $2,000;*

(d) *Pre- and post-judgment interest in accordance with sections 128 and 129 of the Courts of Justice Act, Ontario; and*

(e) *The costs of this action on a solicitor-and-client scale.*

Let's take a closer look at this first paragraph of the claim. Notice that subparagraph (a) provided no information about the nature of the loss for which $5,000 is being claimed. That information will come later. The only time you will specify the injury from which the damages flow is when there are special damages or more than one category. Here's an example of that: Suppose that the home invasion traumatized the minor plaintiff and made it necessary for him to seek supplementary psychological counselling that was not covered by the family's provincial health insurance. In that case, the minor plaintiff would have additional damages to sue for, and these could be outlined in a subsequent paragraph. In order to distinguish the furniture damage relief from the medical expenses relief, you might wish to outline your claim this way:

1. The plaintiffs ... as follows:

(a) General damages for destruction to home furnishings in the amount of $5,000;...

2. The plaintiff Baby Bear further claims special damages in the amount of $2,000 for medical expenses incurred as a result of the defendant's unlawful actions...

Notice that exemplary and punitive damages rated a subparagraph of their own. If the other plaintiffs had been seeking special (medical) damages, they too would have had a subparagraph of their own. Another subparagraph was devoted to a claim for pre- and post-judgment interest, and finally another one for costs. Theoretically, you don't have to seek interest and costs, since they flow automatically in a judgment — but why take chances? Always ask for them.

Now that the damages sought have been spelled out, it's time to provide the facts on which the claim is based. To accomplish this economically and clearly, we suggest you use the old journalistic principle of the "five ws": *who, what, when, where,* and *why.* Start with the *who:*

3. At all material times, the plaintiffs were homeowners residing in the real property municipally known as 10 Forest Animal Lane, Queen City, Ontario.

4. At all material times, the defendant was a resident of Princessville, Ontario and was unknown to the plaintiffs.

The expression "at all materials times" answers the question *when,* but its main purpose is to paint the circumstances that were in existence at the time the tort was committed. It may well be that, later on, the defendant's daughter could end up marrying the child plaintiff and that she could become a frequent and honoured guest in the plaintiff's home. None of that, however, is important to the main issue in this lawsuit, namely that the parties lived in different neighbourhoods and didn't know each other at the time the tort was committed. It is also implicit that the defendant had no business with the plaintiffs that would give her any right to enter their home, an important fact in establishing the requirements of the trespass.

The next "w" question to be answered is *when:*

5. On June 5, 1999, at approximately 9:30 a.m., the defendant entered the home of the plaintiffs while they were away. The defendant had no colour of right to enter the home, nor to utilize any of the furnishings found in it. Despite this, the defendant consumed a quantity of the plaintiffs' food, broke one of their living room chairs, and generally disarranged the plaintiffs' bedrooms. The details of how the chair was broken are best known to the *defendant. The replacement cost of the broken chair, a Louis XIV antique, was $5,000.*

(6) As a consequence of the defendant's trespass, the minor plaintiff Baby Bear suffered severe emotional trauma, treatment of which required psychotherapy and other counselling services. Some of these treatments were not covered by the family's provincial health insurance, and had to be borne by the plaintiffs personally. The cost of these out-of-pocket expenses totalled $2,000.

In two paragraphs, you have summarized the defendant's wrongdoings and the plaintiffs' damages. The defendant committed those three acts (all of them tortious) and did so "without colour of right". That is a very useful expression, because all of us may one day be invited to somebody's home and end up eating their food and accidentally breaking their furniture. In some homes, we may even disarrange their bedrooms if we are lucky. As long as we have colour of right to be there, we won't have to keep an eye out for the process servers.

You will notice that our clients, the plaintiffs, were unable to give us any great details on how the damage came to be done. This is why we wrote that the details were "best known to the defendant." It doesn't matter how the damaged occurred, of course, because no matter what the defendant did, it created an actionable tort.

We have now answered the *who, what* and *when*. Now it is time to address the *why*. In a pleading, the *why* is the law. Question: What law did the defendant break? Answer: The criminal law. Specifically, the defendant's home invasion was a violation of a certain section of the Criminal Code of Canada. We should mentioned this, so let's modify paragraph 5 of our claim:

5. On June 5, 1999, at approximately 9:30 a.m., the defendant entered the home of the plaintiffs while they were away. The defendant had no colour of right to enter the home, nor to utilize any of the furnishings found in it, and her unauthorized entry constituted break-and-enter, contrary to section 348 of the Criminal Code of Canada...

Since we have included a claim for punitive damages, some mention should be made of this in the statement of claim. As you may know, there is no specific statute which covers the parameters for an award of punitive damages. Punitive damages are a common law remedy, and the guidelines for their award are dictated by case law. To this end, whenever your client is seeking punitive damages, it would be a smart idea to do a quick check of the current standards for awarding them. At this writing, *Walker v. D'Arcy* (1999), 117 O.A.C. 367 is a useful case on punitive damages.

Anticipating your later arguments in court, you should take a single principle or sentence from one of these decisions and draft that on to your statement of claim. Let's try this phrase from the *Walker* case:

*7. The unlawful actions of the defendant were so egregious as to be "repre-
hensible and malicious". Accordingly, the plaintiffs are seeking an award of
$50,000 in exemplary and punitive damages.*

Every province and territory has its own specific requirements for
what must be included in a statement of claim. If the plaintiffs in this
action lived in Ontario, they would add the following:

*8. Should a trial of this action be necessary, the plaintiffs ask that it take
place in Kapuskasing.*

The proposed place of trial is almost always the same jurisdiction where
the claim itself is filed.

SAMPLE CLAIM #2

Let's look at another statement of claim, this time in the corporate sphere.
In this action, you represent a Canadian corporation, Jamesco, in a
distribution dispute against an American multinational, Tedco:

STATEMENT OF CLAIM

1. Jamesco Products Inc. ("Jamesco") claims:

(a) *A declaration that the plaintiff is the exclusive distributor in Canada of
Tedco products as hereinafter defined;*

(b) *Damages in an amount as yet unknown but estimated to be $600,000 for
breach of fiduciary duty, reckless or negligent misrepresentation and
unjust enrichment;*

(c) *Damages for loss of business opportunity in an amount as yet unknown
but estimated to be $600,000;*

(d) *An accounting to determine all monies received by the defendants, directly or indirectly, beneficially or otherwise, from, arising out of, or in
association with the sale of Tedco products in Canada;*

(e) *Judgment in accordance with the said accounting;*

(f) *A declaration that some or all of those monies referred to in paragraph (e)
above are trust monies held in trust for the benefit of and for the plaintiff
herein to the extent of the value of its claims in the action;*

(g) *An Order tracing any assets, real or personal property or monies paid,
transferred, taken, removed, received, converted, stolen or misappropriated by the defendants, or any one or more or all of them, either alone or*

in conjunction with one or more other individuals, corporations, part-
nerships, proprietorships or business;

(h) Punitive, exemplary and aggravated damages in the amount of
$200,000;

(i) Pre-judgment and post-judgment interest in accordance with the provisions of the [applicable Rules of Practice];

(j) Its costs of this action on a solicitor-and-client scale;

(k) Such further and other relief as this honourable court may deem just.

2. Jamesco is a body corporate and is engaged in the business of developing
sales opportunities in Canada and elsewhere.

3. The defendant Tedco USA Inc. is a corporation incorporated pursuant to
the laws of the United States and is the corporation responsible for the global
distribution of the Tedco teddy bear, a talking mechanical and electronic
child's toy, together with related toys ("Tedco products").

4. The defendant Tedco Co. (pty) Ltd. and Tedco Industries Ltd. are corporations incorporated pursuant to the laws of the Republic of Argentina and are
the companies responsible for the development and distribution of Tedco
products.

5. In or about April of 1996, the plaintiff entered into negotiations with the
defendants and/or their agents for the purpose of obtaining distribution rights
to Tedco products in Canada.

6. As a result of the negotiations, the defendants, each of them, made various
representations to Jamesco for the purpose of inducing Jamesco to incur costs
to develop the Canadian market for Tedco products, the particulars of which,
inter alia, are as follows:

(a) That Jamesco was the first and only entity in Canada to order volume
stock and consequently Jamesco would be favoured in terms of the sale
and distribution of the Tedco products in Canada;

(b) The defendants would ensure that there would be no crossover between
parties approached with respect to distribution of Tedco products in
Canada;

(c) That the defendants would be interested in building a long-term relationship with Jamesco with respect to distribution of the Tedco products.

7. Jamesco says that it relied upon the foregoing representations to its detriment, as more particularly set out below.

Note that Jamesco's claim is based on the principle of detrimental
reliance. A judge could well figure that out him- or herself, but, being a

good legal writer, you will spell it out explicitly in your statement of claim.

8. Jamesco says a long-term distribution agreement was agreed to by Jamesco and the defendants, which had no fixed term but was to subsist for two years or more.

9. Jamesco further, or in the alternative, alleges that the defendants made the aforesaid representations which:

(a) Were untrue;

(b) They knew or ought to have known were untrue;

(c) Were intended by the defendants to induce Jamesco to act upon the same;

(d) Jamesco relied upon the misrepresentations of the defendants in incurring substantial costs to develop the Canadian market for distribution of Tedco products, to the full knowledge of the defendants;

(e) Jamesco states that, had the defendants not made the foregoing misrepresentations, or, alternatively, had they complied with their duty to bargain and negotiate in good faith, and honestly advise Jamesco of the true status of the distributorship right in Canada, or had the defendants made full disclosure to Jamesco, Jamesco never would have incurred the costs to develop the Canadian market for Tedco products.

Misrepresentation is the basis for the detrimental reliance claim, and so it, too, should be stated explicitly.

10. Jamesco says that in or about early 1998, the defendants abruptly, wrongfully and without cause terminated their relationship with Jamesco.

BREACH OF DUTY

11. Jamesco says that by reason of its position as global distributors of Tedco products, and with the knowledge of the defendants that Jamesco would be incurring substantial costs to develop the Canadian market for Tedco products, the defendants owed to Jamesco a fiduciary duty to act honestly and in good faith and not to Jamesco's detriment.

12. By reason of all of the foregoing, Jamesco says that the defendants breached their fiduciary duty to Jamesco.

13. Furthermore, Jamesco alleges that the defendants owed to Jamesco a fiduciary duty to act in good faith in an honest, frank and forthright manner with respect to the distributorship position of Jamesco in Canada.

14. The defendants breached their duty, did not act in good faith, honestly or frankly, acted in their own interest to the detriment of Jamesco, and accordingly breached their fiduciary duty to Jamesco.

15. Jamesco says that by reason of the defendants' breach of fiduciary duty, they must, in law, disgorge all profits or monies they obtained as a result or consequence relating to or connected with such breach and pay same to Jamesco. Jamesco asks for an accounting to calculate such profit or monies.

We have now moved into another aspect of the tort committed by Tedco against Jamesco — breach of fiduciary duty. Naturally, those words will be embodied in the claim.

16. Jamesco says that the defendants, in wrongfully terminating the exclusive distributorship of Jamesco, unjustly enriched themselves and others at the expense of Jamesco.

17. In law and equity, the defendants must pay in damages, those monies or assets with respect to which they were unjustly enriched, to Jamesco.

Unjust enrichment is another established basis for a claim. Remember: In legal circles, travelling the well-worn path is usually the best route to take.

LOSS OF BUSINESS OPPORTUNITY

18. As set out above, Jamesco would never have had incurred the substantial costs to develop the Canadian market for Tedco products had the defendants been honest and forthright.

19. By reason of the defendants' dishonesty, misrepresentations and actions, and the defendants' knowledge of same, Jamesco was deprived of an opportunity of continuing, carrying on, and fostering the development of its business with respect to distribution of Tedco products in Canada.

20. But for the actions of the defendants, Jamesco would have continued to carry on business and earn significant profits. Jamesco alleges that, in law, the defendants are responsible for the damages and the lost opportunity to earn to profits. Jamesco requests an accounting to determine such loss and judgment in accordance with such accounting.

TRUST CLAIM

21. Furthermore, to the extent that the defendants directly or indirectly received any monies that were diverted or misappropriated as a result of the termination of their relationship with Jamesco, then such monies constitute trust monies to stand to the credit of and for the benefit of Jamesco.

22. Jamesco requests an accounting in this regard and an Order tracing any such monies so illegally misappropriated by the defendants, together with judgment in accordance with such accounting and tracing and a declaration that such monies are trust monies, held for the benefit and credit, inter alia, Jamesco.

PUNITIVE DAMAGES

23. Jamesco says that the actions of the defendants, particularized above, were done intentionally by them, in complete, total and utter disregard to Jamesco's rights, contractual, legal, equitable and otherwise, and furthermore that the defendants' actions in this regard are heinous, outrageous, high-handed and in total and complete abuse of their respective positions and, accordingly, Jamesco says that the defendants must pay to it significant punitive, aggravated and exemplary damages in the sum of $200,000.

24. Jamesco says that it is entitled to damages in the sum of $600,000. Jamesco does not, at this time, have full particulars of the damages that have been suffered by way of the defendants' wrongful and illegal conduct.

25. Jamesco says that it will, prior to trial of this action, provide particulars of the damages that it has suffered.

26. This statement of claim is served upon the defendants pursuant to [the applicable Rules of Practice] as, among other things, the contractual and tortious relationships between the parties were created in Kapuskasing and the damages suffered were in Kapuskasing.

We will look at statements of defence and defence issues in the next chapter.

Chapter 4

STATEMENTS OF DEFENCE

INTRODUCTION

In the last chapter, we explored statements of claim. The statement of claim is the first shot fired in the war that constitutes a lawsuit. In this chapter, we will look at "shots" fired by the other side — statements of defence.

A statement of defence fulfills many functions. Like a statement of claim, it is an opportunity to create a good first impression. More specifically, it presents the trier of fact with a first impression of your side of the case and the merits of your case. Obviously you want to make that first impression a good one.

Statements of defence are very precise in the way they are designed. This structure is the same no matter what the case is about, and these limitations are actually beneficial, both to you and to the trier of fact reading them. Statements of defence are divided into four parts:

1. Admissions;
2. Denials;
3. Identification of issues that the defence knows nothing about; and
4. The defence's version of the facts of the case.

It should also be noted that there are a number of specific legal arguments which, if you plan to use them, must be pleaded in your statement of defence. If you fail to plead them right off the bat, you may be barred from doing so later on. (Try explaining that error to the client!)

The first three elements just listed are pretty straightforward, and they are all laid out in a standard format. Let's look at a statement of defence for the following claim:

CLAIM

1. The plaintiff, Fefi Fofum, claims from the defendant, Jack Beanplanter:

(a) General damages in the amount of $12,517.22;

    (b) *Special and aggravated damages in the amount of $5,641.99;*

    (c) *Punitive damages in the amount of $5,000;*

    (d) *Pre- and post-judgment interest in accordance with sections 128 and 129 of the Courts of Justice Act; and*

    (e) *The costs of this action on a solicitor-and-client scale.*

2. At all material times, the plaintiff was a resident of Cloudtown, in the Regional Municipality of Troposphere. He was the owner of the real property municipally known as 1 Castle Drive, Cloudtown.

3. At all material times, the defendant was a resident of Garbanza, in the Municipality of Poorland.

4. On or about May 30, 2000, the defendant trespassed on the plaintiff's property and entered his home. The plaintiff did not give the defendant permission to perform either of these acts.

5. While in the plaintiff's home, the defendant took without colour of right a golden egg, which was the property of the plaintiff. He then left the plaintiff's home and returned to his own residence, carrying the egg with him. The egg's value is estimated at $1,200.

6. On or about May 31, 2000, the day following the theft described above, the defendant returned to the plaintiff's property and again entered his home without permission. On this second occasion, the plaintiff was at home and, solely in the interest of protecting his family and preserving his personal property, he chased the defendant around the house. Had he caught the defendant, the plaintiff would have detained him pending the arrival of the police.

7. In the ensuing chase, while he attempted to escape lawful arrest, the defendant knocked over a painting by A.Y. Jackson, owned by the plaintiff, causing damage to it in the amount of $5,000.

8. As he was leaving the plaintiff's home, the defendant took without colour of right a specially bred Yukon Goldrush hen, valued at $1,125.00.

9. The defendant also took, again without colour of right, a Loman/Forrester singing harp, valued at $1,125.00.

10. During the pursuit, the plaintiff had occasion to climb onto an organic ladder which the defendant had grown expressly for the purpose of trespassing on the plaintiff's property. While the plaintiff was climbing down this ladder, the defendant severed its bottom layer, thereby causing the plaintiff to fall a distance of 10 meters to the ground. As a result of this fall, the plaintiff cracked his right fibula and experienced considerable bruising and pain to other parts of his body.

11. As our society values the sanctity of the home and condemns those who would breach it, the plaintiff seeks a denouncement of the defendant's double invasion by an award of punitive damages.

12. If this matter should go to trial, the plaintiff asks that it be held in Yellowknife.

Dated: August 2, 2000

Boop Boop Adoop
Barristers and Solicitors
23 Skidoo Avenue, 19th Floor
Thunder Bay, Ontario
P7B 5L7

I.M.A. Notherloyyur
(807)555-2349
(807)555-9432 Fax

Solicitor for the Plaintiff

Naturally, when this client comes to you, he will tell you that he is pure as the driven snow. As his counsel, you will, of course, believe him, or at least conduct yourself on the basis that the client is, indeed, innocent. You will then set about constructing a defence for this client. Let's put together a statement of defence, using the four-part formula:

ADMISSIONS

Here's an important rule that applies to statements of defence in every jurisdiction: Your statement of defence should address every point in the statement of claim. This is especially important because if you don't deal with a particular point in the statement of claim, it is assumed to be true! Bearing in mind that most statements of claim contain damaging allegations, it is essential that you not let a single point go by undealt with!

Paragraph 1 of your statement of defence deals with admissions. There are usually a few things in the plaintiff's claim that you don't mind admitting are true. Just begin your defence by listing them according to the paragraph order of the statement of claim:

DEFENCE

1. The defendant admits the allegations contained in paragraphs 1, 3, 4 (to the extent that he was present on the property in question on the day in question), 5 (to the extent that he had in his possession the golden egg referred to), 6 (again, to the extent that he was present on the property in question, and that the plaintiff pursued him), 8 (to the extent that he had in his possession the hen referred to), and 9 (to the extent that he had in his possession the harp referred to) of the statement of claim.

You are, of course, agreeing with the first paragraph, since there's no doubt that the plaintiff is suing you. You also agree that your client lives in Garbanza. As you may have noticed, a number of the paragraphs in the statement of claim made allegations which (according to your client) were partly true and partly untrue. Proper form dictates that you list the parts you do agree with in the admissions paragraph of your statement of defence.

DENIALS

The parts you don't agree with are listed in the denials paragraph, which comes next:

> 2. *The defendant denies the allegations contained in paragraphs 4 (to the extent that he knowingly trespassed), 5 (to the extent that his taking the golden egg was an act of theft), 8 (to the extent that his taking the hen was an act of theft), 9 (to the extent that his taking the harp was an act of theft), and 10 (to the extent that the "organic ladder" was designed expressly for the purpose of facilitating a burglary), of the statement of claim, and puts the plaintiff to the strict proof thereof.*

Here again we selected the portions of each paragraph that are the focus of our denial. As you will see in a minute, the client isn't denying he was there, nor that he took stuff from the plaintiff's home. However, he says, it wasn't a burglary.

Notice also the use of the term of art "and puts the plaintiff to the strict proof thereof." That's a great expression, "strict proof." It is meant to imply a high standard of evidence in proving the allegation. Still, there really isn't another standard of proof in a court of law, is there? Have you ever heard of a lackadaisical defendant putting a plaintiff to the "loosey-goosey proof thereof?"

NO KNOWLEDGE OF

The next paragraph deals with allegations of which the defendant has no knowledge:

> 3. *The defendant has no knowledge of the allegations listed in paragraphs 2, 5 (to the extent of the value of the golden egg), 6 (to the extent of the plaintiff's state of mind or motives at that point in time), 7, 8 (to the extent of the value of the hen), 9 (to the extent of the value of the harp), and 10 (to the extent of the plaintiff's injuries, if any).*

A lot of inexperienced counsel make a very human mistake when drafting the "no knowledge" paragraphs of their statements of defence. It is normal for people to fill in grey areas in their understanding of a situation with hypothesis and supposition; it is not normal for a person to admit that he or she doesn't know something. Want an example? You're going to be taking a train somewhere and there's a scheduled one-hour stopover at lunchtime in a train station along the way. Your travelling companion asks "What will be able to buy for lunch there?" and you automatically answer "Oh, hamburgers, sandwiches, candy, chips..." even if you've never been to that station. You didn't phone up in advance, of course, but your knowledge and previous experience fill in that knowledge gap with a reasonable supposition of what you're likely to find at the Terminal Diner. Well, that technique works fine for guesses at *cuisine de la gare*, but you should avoid it in pleadings. Unless you know something, say you don't know it. No one will take you to task for it and, even if they do, how are they going to prove what's inside your brain? Short of asking Mr. Spock to perform a Vulcan mind-meld, there's no way.

Take a look at paragraph 3 in our statement of defence. The plaintiff tried to sneak a characterization of himself as stout-hearted defender of the family home. You don't know for certain that he wasn't, but remember that every allegation you ignore is considered to be admitted. Therefore, we simply state that the defendant has no knowledge of a whole list of things, and the ball is back in the plaintiff's court to prove them.

THE DEFENDANT'S VERSION OF THE FACTS

Once we've gotten the three obligatory paragraphs out of the way, it's time to tell the story from the defendant's point of view. What you'll say here, of course, depends on what your client tells you and instructs you to write. There will be cases where, despite your most eloquent begging, the client insists that you commit to paper a very silly and ineffective statement of defence. This is the client's privilege, of course, and your primary obligations in those circumstances are not to knowingly plead a falsehood, and also to be sure you have a sizeable retainer in your trust account.

Usually, however, your client will have a defence to the plaintiff's claim that can, at least, survive preliminary scrutiny. Let's see what Mr. Beanplanter has to say in this case:

4. At all material times, the defendant was employed as a bailiff and private investigator, in the employ of the Reallybig Insurance Company of Canada ("the insurance company").

5. In January 2000, the defendant was retained by the insurance company to locate and repossess various valuable items which had been stolen from the Red River Museum in Winnipeg ("the museum"). Included among these stolen items were the hen and harp referred to in the statement of claim.

6. After completing thorough investigation, the defendant arrived at the reasonable conclusion that the hen and harp in question were the property of the museum or, in the alternative, the insurance company by subrogation. Regardless, the defendant concluded that the plaintiff had no colour of right to them.

7. Relying on his statutory and common law authority as a bailiff, the defendant took steps to lawfully repossess the hen and harp. In furtherance of this objective, he arranged to clandestinely obtain a sample golden egg for the sole purpose of comparing its gold isotopes with the isotopes known to have been prominent in the golden eggs of the stolen hen.

8. *After laboratory tests confirmed the virtual certainty that the golden egg from the plaintiff's home had, in fact, originated with the stolen hen, the defendant took steps to lawfully enter the plaintiff's residence to reclaim the museum's stolen property. Accordingly, on or about May 30, 2000, he entered the plaintiff's home and found the plaintiff there. Thereupon, the defendant identified himself as a bailiff and agent of the insurance company, and announced to the plaintiff that he was in possession of stolen property which, by right of statute, he was forthwith repossessing.*

9. *Rather than accede to the defendant's lawful request, the plaintiff became violent and attempted to injure the defendant. Fearing for his safety, the defendant fled, despite which the plaintiff continued to follow him even after he had left the plaintiff's premises.*

10. *The defendant repeats that he has no knowledge or recollection of the damage alleged to have been done to the plaintiff's painting. Even if he did damage it (which is not admitted but expressly denied), the defendant states that said painting was accidentally damaged while he was fleeing from the plaintiff's unlawful attack, but for which the accident never would have happened.*

11. *The defendant repeats that he has no knowledge of the plaintiff injuring himself by falling from an "organic ladder". Even if the plaintiff was injured (which is not admitted but expressly denied), the defendant states that said injury was caused by the plaintiff's unlawful pursuit of the defendant, but for which the injury never would have happened.*

12. *The defendant states that the plaintiff's losses and/or injuries (which are not admitted but expressly denied) are exaggerated and excessive. Additionally, or in the alternative, they were preventable by the plaintiff, and/or the plaintiff could have taken steps to mitigate his losses or injuries.*

13. *The defendant further states that all of his actions were lawful in the context of his position as bailiff and private investigator, and grant him statutory protection from prosecution or liability in tort.*

14. *The defendant pleads and relies on the Private Investigator's Protective Act, R.S.O. 1990 c. P.5, as amended.*

15. *The defendant asks that the plaintiff's claim be dismissed with costs.*

Dated: August 24, 2000

Peter Piecedebouche
Barrister and Solicitor
403 Maple Street
Sudbury, Ontario
P3C 2B1

(705)555-9102
(705)555-2718 Fax

Solicitor for the Defendant

Several points are worth noting: There were several instances where the defendant found himself in the awkward position of dealing with allegations that he was denying ever took place. He got around that in places like paragraph 11 by repeating his denial and lack of knowledge, and then going on to say that *even if those things happened*, the defendant was not responsible. In fact, the pleading went a step further by using the bracketed words "which is not admitted but expressly denied". It's a little stuffy-sounding, but it makes the defendant's point crystal clear. It also reinforces the underlying message "This guy doesn't know what he's talking about in his pleading".

Another thing to note is the citation of a helpful statute. This (fictitious) statute is being relied on by the defendant to shield him from liability for his actions. Needless to say, this is something that better be pleaded, or else it can't be brought up later on.

The final paragraph, asking for the claim to be dismissed with costs, is *de rigeur*, and it also happens to be the item at the top of the defendant's wish list. It should always be included.

OTHER ITEMS TO INCLUDE

As mentioned earlier, statements of defence have a few more requirements and rules than do statements of claim. There's still ample room for creativity and thoroughness, despite these requirements, but you have to be careful you fulfill them. Never forget: If the plaintiff claims something and you don't defend it properly, it's deemed to have been admitted. This is an "error and omission" — in the most painful sense of the phrase!

Let's look at some items that have to be specifically pleaded if you're going to rely on them. Note our use of the word "some" — this is not an exhaustive list. For the purposes of this overview, we'll stick to the Ontario Rules of Civil Procedure, although these are matters are found in the civil litigation rules of every province:

STATUTES

As we saw above, a statute deprives a plaintiff of the right to claim certain issues:

Illegality

As the old expression goes, "you can't come to court with dirty hands". If the basis of the plaintiff's claim is itself illegal, that's a good defence — provided you plead it.

Jurisdiction

The court in which the plaintiff is seeking relief doesn't have jurisdiction to deal with the matter.

Contributory Negligence

The plaintiff's own conduct was responsible for his damages. (See paragraphs 10 and 11 of our statement of defence.)

Limitations

A statutory limitation period makes it too late for the plaintiff to sue.

Insanity

The defendant who breached a contract was mentally ill at the time he or she signed it, and the plaintiff knew this.

Res Judicata

The matter has already been litigated and a final ruling has been made.

Settled Account

The (presumably unpaid) account that forms the basis of the plaintiff's claim was, in fact, settled.

Waiver

The plaintiff previously gave a waiver to the defendant permitting the conduct which later became the basis for the plaintiff's claim.

Remember: The above is not an exhaustive list. There may be other defences, which the local rules may require you to plead *ab initio* if you intend to rely on them. Check your rules.

SET-OFF

Set-off is a defence. As a procedural matter, a claim for set-off is very powerful as it allows the defendant to raise, against an otherwise unbeatable claim, a procedurally and substantively valid defence, which can require the plaintiff to take a claim through to trial and can avoid procedural shortcuts to judgment, such as summary judgment.[1] In effect,

---

[1]   Of course, the shrewd plaintiff will move for partial summary judgment on all issues but the set-off, and seek immediately enforcement; *Neiman v. Edward* (1987), 17 C.P.C. (2d) 133 (Ont. Dist. Ct.).

set-off allows a defendant to put a hidden claim in the body of the defence. Indeed, if the set-off claim exceeds the claim, at least for legal set-off, judgment may be granted to the defendant.

As a matter of law, set-off is quite limited. Nevertheless, in any case where it is even faintly plausible that the plaintiff is obliged to the defendant, a plea of set-off is prudent. The bald plea is as follows:

> *The defendant pleads and relies on the doctrines of legal and equitable set-off and asks the court to grant judgment for the surplus of monies due from the plaintiff to the defendant over those, if any due from the defendant to the plaintiff.*

Surprisingly, plaintiffs seldom move to have a claim of set-off dismissed as being insufficient at law. They should. Set-off is seldom available and, as a substantive defence, can delay a plaintiff significantly by raising numerous collateral issues only loosely linked to the claim.

In order properly to plead set-off, sufficient material facts to justify legal or equitable set-off must be put in the defence. Legal set-off applies only if (1) the claim and the set-off are both debts, and (2) are mutual cross-obligations. Only liquidated sums or money demands reducible to a sum certain can be set-off against each other at law.[2] Obviously, very few genuine cases of legal set-off will arise.

Sometimes you may not have a genuine set-off, but there may still be an argument to be made that some matter requires relief to flow from the plaintiff to the defendant. In that case, you can often plead *equitable set-off*. Equitable set-off gives a broader scope for defendants, but even here the set-off claimed can only apply if it is an obligation so closely bound to the claim that it would be unconscionable to allow the claim to proceed without the set-off.[3] Equitable set-off does not require the obligations be liquidated to a sum certain. Broadly put, equitable set-off merely requires that the opposing claims flow from the same transaction or relationship between the parties.[4] Unrelated claims cannot be the subject of legal or equitable set-off;[5] however, language may be used in a defence to obscure the factual *lacunae*. Such language might include:

> *The claim and the obligation of the plaintiff to the defendant, for which set-off at law and equity is pleaded, arise from the same relationship and series of transactions. They flow from the same legal and factual matrix and it would be unconscionable and unequitable to allow the plaintiff's claim to proceed without a consideration of the defendant's legal, equitable and statutory entitlements.*

---

[2]   *Agway Metals Inc. v. Dufferin Roofing Ltd.* (1991), 46 C.P.C. (2d) 133 (Ont. Gen. Div.).

[3]   *Agway Metals Inc. v. Dufferin Roofing Ltd.* (1991), 46 C.P.C. (2d) 133 (Ont. Gen. Div.).

[4]   *H.D. Madden & Associates Inc. v. Brendan Wood, Tutsch, & Partners Inc.* (1989), 33 C.P.C. (2d) 263 (Ont. Dist. Ct.).

[5]   Although they may found a counterclaim.

COUNTERCLAIMS AND CLAIMS OVER

Counterclaims or claims over are similar to claims or defences insofar as they are of substantive merit or not. A counterclaim delivered with a view to obfuscate matters will be drafted in a way that will slow matters down and will plead broadly and without a carefully narrowed focus. By contrast, where judgment on the counterclaim is both a real possibility and desired by the party, a narrowly focused "claim-like" pleading is most appropriate. That said, pleadings carefully tied to the parties and facts make a far more persuasive document.

SAMPLE STATEMENT OF DEFENCE AND CLAIM OVER

Obviously, each proceeding has a different claim and its form has to match the nature of the claim. That said, for illustrative purposes, a sample defence and claim over follows.

STATEMENT OF DEFENCE AND COUNTERCLAIM

1. The defendants admit the allegations contained in paragraphs 6, 7, 9 (as to terms, save that paragraph 3 as reproduced ought to refer to October 31, 1993), 12 (as to quantum but not entitlement), 14 (but states that multiple signatures were required only for cheques in excess of $1,000), 16 (as to date of notice of termination) and 19 of the statement of claim.

2. The defendants deny the remaining allegations contained in the statement of claim.

3. The defendant I.S. Company Limited ("Company") states that it has been improperly named in this proceeding and that its proper name is Irwin Steinberg & Associates Limited.

PARTIES

4. The defendant Jean-Louis Steinberg ("Steinberg") is a businessman carrying on business in the consulting industry with signing authority for Company and I.S. Consulting Limited ("Consulting").

5. The plaintiff Jack Bakemore Consulting is a sole proprietorship of the plaintiff Jack Bakemore.

INITIAL CONTACT

6. In or about September 1990, the plaintiffs' previous company, Amazing Impulse Inc., was in the process of going bankrupt and the plaintiffs approached Company with a view to working with Company, or an affiliated company, as a salesman bringing with them their existing client base.

7. *Company and the plaintiffs agreed, in principle, to the plaintiffs working with Company.*

8. *At all material times, the plaintiffs were engaged in the business of selling and were never held out as being consultants to, and never did consult for, Company or Consulting.*

CONTRACT

9. *On or about May 14, 1993, the plaintiffs and Company executed a commissions agreement, some of the terms of which are reproduced in paragraph 9 of the statement of claim.*

10. *No other contracts were executed by the plaintiffs and any of the defendants. Similarly, no shares in Consulting were transferred to the plaintiffs.*

11. *Nevertheless, draft documentation providing for a transfer of shares in Consulting and the governance of Consulting by way of Unanimous Shareholders Agreement was prepared. The plaintiffs were to obtain clients who would be serviced by the plaintiffs through Consulting. Production of consulting material would be carried out, in large measure, by Company. The plaintiffs, Company and Consulting, governed their relationship by reference to these documents and were bound by them as written memoranda of their verbal agreements.*

12. *The plaintiffs refused to execute the draft documentation, or to accept a transfer of shares in Consulting, stating initially that the bankruptcy of Amazing Impulse Inc. forbade them from executing these documents or accepting the shares. Subsequently, upon repeated request by Consulting and Company that the plaintiffs execute the documents, the plaintiffs, in or about February 1996, expressly and vigorously refused so to do stating that they never intended to execute the documents and that Company and Consulting were sorely mistaken in believing that the plaintiffs would in this way honour their agreement.*

13. *A crucial element of the agreement between the plaintiffs Consulting and Company was that, should the plaintiffs cease working with Consulting and Company, the plaintiffs would not take clients' consulting work brought to Consulting or Company away from Consulting or Company for a period of 12 months. In any event, Consulting states that the plaintiffs were fiduciaries of Consulting and could not compete with, or remove clients from, Consulting for a period of at least 12 months.*

TERMINATION OF AGREEMENTS

14. *On or about January 19, 1996, the plaintiffs, by written notice, terminated the agreements between the plaintiffs, Consulting and Company, effective April 19, 1996.*

15. *In breach of their agreements with Consulting and Company, the plaintiffs, and prior to April 19, 1996, and forthwith after January 19, 1996:*

(a) The plaintiffs removed client files from the offices of Consulting and Company, which files were returned only after threat of legal action;

(b) The plaintiffs took, without prior notice, clients' graphic production work from Consulting and Company to a new consulting firm;

(c) The plaintiffs ceased providing appropriate, or any, services to Consulting or Company and, indeed, expressly refused to fulfill, or even discuss, their contractual obligations to Consulting and Company.

16. Subsequent to leaving Consulting, and well after April 19, 1996, the plaintiffs advised Consulting's banker that Jack Bakemore was president of Consulting and that he should be advised of and give authority for Consulting's banking. These representations were, to the plaintiffs' knowledge, false.

DAMAGE TO CONSULTING AND COMPANY

17. As a result of the plaintiffs' breach of agreement and fiduciary duty with Consulting and Company, these companies have lost profit in an amount presently estimated to be $259,000.

SPECIFIC DENIALS AND RESPONSES TO STATEMENT OF CLAIM

18. Without limiting the generality of the foregoing and especially the denials contained herein, the defendants, each of them, state as follows:

(a) With respect to paragraph 11 of the statement of claim, the shares in Consulting were not transferred to the plaintiffs and, in any event, were owned by Company and not Steinberg. Further, the plaintiffs expressly refused to accept the transfer of shares;

(b) With respect to paragraph 12 of the statement of claim, Consulting states that the plaintiffs' entitlement, which is denied, was, in any event, premised upon Consulting having sufficient net revenue to make the requisite payment. As a result of the wrongful acts of the plaintiffs, Consulting is neither obliged to make the payment alleged nor has the prerequisite revenues for such payment;

(c) With respect to paragraphs 8, 10, 11, 12, 15 and 16 of the statement of claim, neither of the plaintiffs ever entered into contractual, or other legally binding, relations of any sort with Steinberg;

(d) With respect to paragraph 15 of the statement of claim:

    (i) Company personnel were fully qualified and competent and, indeed, often remedied significant problems engendered by neglect or lack of skill of the plaintiffs;

    (ii) Company's production costs were consistent with, or below, market rates;

    (iii) *Company was fully capable of handling, and did handle, the quantity and quality of work produced by the plaintiffs;*

    (iv) *Steinberg was constantly involved with fulfilling his contractual obligations to Company and Consulting, however, Steinberg had no obligations to the plaintiffs;*

    (v) *Company, as previously stated, did not charge excessive rates and, in any event, Steinberg never charged any rates for Consulting's production;*

 (e) *With respect to paragraph 16 of the statement of claim:*

    (i) *There was, and is, no deadlock in the Board of Directors of Consulting;*

    (ii) *Steinberg has not taken over Consulting, rather, as a result of the plaintiffs' wrongful acts, Consulting has no business and is dormant, although still a body corporate in good standing;*

    (iii) *The plaintiffs have never been denied access to the premises of Consulting or Company and, indeed, the plaintiffs neglected or refused to pick up personal property of Jack Bakemore, though asked so to do by the defendants;*

    (iv) *Consulting properly changed its signing authority upon the plaintiffs ceasing to honour their agreement with, inter alia, Consulting;*

    (v) *I.S. is an unknown entity, however, Steinberg never issued any cheques requiring Steinberg's approval without such approval;*

    (vi) *and (vii) Consulting and Company are content that the plaintiffs conduct an independent audit of their books and records and, subject to set-off, will pay any monies due to the plaintiffs.*

SET-OFFS

19. *Consulting and Company plead and rely upon the doctrines of legal and equitable set-off and claim judgment for the amount by which the sums due to them from the plaintiffs exceed the sums, if any, due to the plaintiffs. The claims of the plaintiffs and defendants are closely related and cannot fairly be dealt with one without the other. The defendants plead and rely on the Courts of Justice Act (Ontario), section 111.*

20. *The defendants therefore ask that this action be dismissed with costs.*

COUNTERCLAIM

21. *Company and Consulting claim against the plaintiffs:*

(a) *Damages in an amount as yet unquantified but presently estimated to be $259,000;*

(b) *Pre- and post-judgment interest pursuant to the Courts of Justice Act;*

(c) *Costs; and*

(d) *Such further and other relief as to this Honourable Court seems fit.*

22. *Company and Consulting repeat and rely upon the facts set forth in the defence herein.*

LANGUAGE AND STYLE

Before concluding this chapter, a word on language and style is appropriate. A temperate tone is always the appropriate tone for all legal writing, but the type of language used within the spectrum of the temperate is governed by the nature of the case. When acting for a plaintiff in a straightforward case where the law and common sense coincide with the facts, a narrowly focused, short pleading drafted in concrete, personal language is best. By contrast, when acting for unsavory defendants whose best hopes lie with confusion of their complex and confusing delicts, a diffuse, impersonal and somewhat complex pleading may be more effective. I emphasize that there is no single style for writing pleadings, and that which suits one case may not suit another. The very same language can have differing impact and meaning depending on the context — recognize this and govern yourself accordingly.

Chapter 5

MOTIONS AND APPLICATIONS

INTRODUCTION

If your professional goal is to become a courtroom lawyer, then motions and applications will be your staple diet. The glamour of advocacy will come at trial, where you can indulge in all the hysterics and histrionics it takes to get you labeled either a brilliant advocate or just a nutbar. But trial work is the very occasional reward at the end of a long road, and, these days, you will find yourself visiting there less and less often. The reason is simple: Trials are expensive and time-consuming. Even if you're lucky to find a client who can afford a trial, you'll find that the courts don't have the resources, and the system will do everything it can to coerce you into settling.

This is where motions and applications come in. Once you realize that a good settlement is the ultimate outcome, the focus shifts to manoeuvring your side into the best position at negotiation time. Each motion and application is a miniature battle in a larger war. Motions and applications don't win the war, but each victory can move your clients a step closer to what they want.

Motions, of course, are won on two fronts: There is the brilliant verbal advocacy you give before the judge, which is perhaps 25 per cent of the equation. The remaining 75 per cent consists of your preparation, which has at its core cogent and clearly written advocacy. Written motion rules all revolve around one basic principle: Whichever party lays out its side of the story in the clearest and most concise fashion is the party that stands the best chance of getting what it wants from the judge. It's often that simple.

PITY THE JUDGE

Most counsel don't feel empathy for the judges they argue in front of. If their side wins, the person on the bench is someone who can see clearly, "put two and two together", and who has made the only possible decision given the obvious facts. If their side loses, the judge is a nincompoop, blind to the truth, and probably only got appointed because he or she knew somebody in the Attorney General's office. Win or lose, counsel expect the judicial officer to read their motion materials from cover to cover, thoughtfully chew over what they've read, listen to insightful arguments from counsel, and dispense the wrath of God (plus costs on a solicitor-and-client scale).

The reality, of course, is anything but this fantasy. The average judge arrives at court each day to find a docket of 50 motions to be heard, each with an estimated time of 45 minutes. His Honour was only assigned to a particular courtroom that morning and hasn't even read the morning paper, never mind the motion records. Somehow, a judge will convince 40 cases to adjourn or settle, and then will plunge into hearing the rest, with one very important instruction to counsel: Be quick, be concise, be clear, and, as much as possible, lead me by the hand down the road you want me to travel. Deviate and you're done for.

Now that you've been warned, let's look at how to draft written materials that will put you in the courtroom winner's circle.

FORMAL RULES FOR MOTIONS

The formal requirements for motions are set out in the relevant rules of practice. Regardless of the exact format required in your province, all motions require a notice of motion.

The notice of motion sets out for the court what precise relief you're seeking, the grounds for that relief, and the evidence that will be used to support the grounds. This evidence, of course, is written; *viva voce* evidence is almost never allowed in motions court. In most situations, affidavits in support of the motion will be required, although on occasion the affidavit will be unnecessary,[1] or the relevant rules may allow for motions without affidavits.[2] For particularly important motions, a factum may be required as a part of the motion; factums are dealt with elsewhere in this book, so we won't discuss them much in this chapter.

The notice of motion should be a self-contained document which, while referring to other material, makes sense by itself.

SPECIAL CONSIDERATIONS FOR SUMMARY JUDGMENT MOTIONS

Today's courts stop just short of threatening death to convince counsel to avoid trial. Summary judgment is a very attractive way to accomplish

---

[1]   For example, a motion to dismiss a civil claim for failure to assert a cause of action: *Trendsetter Developments Ltd. v. Ottawa Financial Corp.* (1989), 33 C.P.C. (2d) 16 (Ont. C.A.).

[2]   Some case management systems generally rely on counsel to set out uncontested facts from which the court can grant relief.

this goal. Summary judgment is a weapon designed to get rid of claims or defences that have no substantive merit. A bogus defence or claim can now be eliminated without the need for trial, provided there is no genuine issue for trial.[3] The need to show that there is no genuine issue makes summary judgment difficult. It is not sufficient merely to show that your case is stronger than the party opposite's case. You have to convince a judge that there is no case to decide.

What exactly is a "genuine issue for trial?" Essentially, when some area is in dispute and could affect the final decision of the whole trial, it's a genuine issue for trial. If there is a real possibility that this issue may be decided in favour of one side early in the process, go for summary judgment. Accordingly, when drafting materials for a summary judgment motion, you should focus on the points in dispute and emphasize how these disputes are more apparent than real. For example, there may be a real dispute as to fact, but it's immaterial if it relates to unimportant matters. (Nobody cares if the defendant's car struck the crippled plaintiff at 100 km. per hour or 120 km. per hour.) Other disputes of fact may be relevant but clearly unreal. (The trustee of an art collection who is accused of disposing of the artworks may argue that they were, in fact, beamed aboard a passing starship. Unless the presiding judge is a Romulan, however, this defence will be punted early on.) Of course, if you're trying to avoid summary judgment, your materials have to emphasize how many genuine unresolved issues really do exist.

Since a failed motion for summary judgment leads to a great waste of time and money, and causes considerable delay, care should be taken before bringing a motion for judgment. Do not move unless you are fairly sure of success.

JURISDICTION OF THE COURT

It is usually fairly obvious who has jurisdiction to hear a motion. For example, a provincial court judge hearing a preliminary inquiry does not have jurisdiction to stay a criminal proceeding for unreasonable delay.[4] Similarly, a master cannot determine a novel point of law.[5] In such cases, where there is no option, the court where the motion is brought poses no issue.

You will sometimes find, however, that more than one level of court has jurisdiction to hear a motion — a situation that forces you to decide where to bring your motion. Your decision must take into account your

---

[3] *Hercules Managements Ltd. v. Ernst & Young*, [1997] 2 S.C.R. 165.
[4] *Mills v. The Queen*, [1986] 1 S.C.R. 863.
[5] *A.G. England v. Royal Bank of Canada*, [1948] O.W.N. 782 (H.C.).

experience with the type of hearing likely available[6] and the effect that your choice of jurisdiction will have on appeal routes.[7] That said, as a general rule, it is most effective to bring motions before the lowest level of court having jurisdiction.

The lowest level court with jurisdiction is the court that customarily hears the relevant motion. As a general rule, it is best that the form of your legal documents is familiar to the court; to ensure this, choose the customary court for that type of motion. Further, more senior courts often resent dealing with matters that could have been dealt with by a lower level. Nevertheless, if there is a good reason to move before a higher court (say, a refusal motion that involves arguable legal issues), bring your motion to the higher court. In any event, regardless of what level of court is chosen, explicitly state somewhere in the notice of motion why you have chosen that jurisdiction.

PRECISE RELIEF SOUGHT

The central focus of a motion is the relief sought. Accordingly, it is to the "relief sought" that the judge hearing the motion turns. If this section is unclear or overly broad, the judge will be immediately dismayed. It is helpful to narrow the focus of the motion as much as possible. Courts seldom grant more relief than absolutely necessary and an overly broad claim will strike the court hearing the motion as seeking excessive relief. An overly broad claim for relief is unpersuasive and weakens the motion.

A typical example of an overly broad claim for relief sought is where a party, on a motion for an order compelling answers for questions refused, asks that a pleading be struck. Such relief is never granted and, in light of what is actually needed (an order to reattend and answer questions), is wildly excessive. A judge reading such "relief sought" is likely to dismiss the remainder of the material as of little worth. Using the same example, on many discoveries, quite a few refusals are made; some of which are proper and some of which are not. Moving for an order to reattend and answer all the questions weakens the motion. Only those questions that can legitimately be required ought to be moved on. A good rule is not to seek relief that will not be granted.

In limiting the relief sought to that which may plausibly be given, you should consider seeking alternative relief. For example, in seeking summary judgment, an alternative might be judgment with a reference for damages, or an order that trial proceed forthwith on limited issues.

---

[6]   For example, if a master can hear a motion, but, for systemic issues it is unlikely the
      master will be able to consider the motion carefully, it may be better to take the motion
      to a judge.
[7]   There is usually an automatic right of appeal from a master; such rights may be limited
      if the appeal is from a judge.

The advantage of seeking alternative relief is two-fold. First, careful alternatives show the judge that you have considered the options fully, making your materials more credible. Second, judges like compromise. If you give a judge an option that appears to "split the difference" between the parties, the court may well go with that option. A stark "all or nothing" choice may lead to precisely nothing in return. This second advantage of claiming alternative relief can, however, also be a disadvantage. If you need, and are entitled to, certain relief, and give the judge an option of granting less than that relief, the judge may give you less than you need. It is important not to propose any relief that you really cannot live with.

Usually the relief sought concludes with a claim for costs and "such further relief as counsel may advise and this honourable court accept". The claim for costs ought to be given consideration in the context of the motion. If, for example, an indulgence of the court is sought (say, setting aside a default), consider explicitly stating that costs are not sought. The failure to seek costs will stand out and, by being eminently reasonable, will lend credit to your motion. Simply asking that costs be in the event of the cause is unusual enough to make the judge consider your material more closely. Of course, where costs are appropriate and proper, do seek costs.

Occasionally a complaint is raised about the basket provision[8] claim for relief in a notice of motion. Granted, such a basket provision usually does very little and merely adds text to the notice of motion. Further, in a properly drawn motion it is unlikely that any need for the basket provision exists. All that said, there is little real downside to including the basket provision and it provides some protection in the event that, as the responding materials are delivered, somewhat different relief from that originally sought becomes appropriate. In that situation, the basket provision can be tied to a factum and any specific relief that may differ from the relief set out in the notice of motion can be explicitly set out in the factum.

GROUNDS FOR RELIEF

As mentioned previously, a notice of motion ought to be a self-contained document that can be read and understood without reading other material. Accordingly, the grounds for the relief sought should briefly set out enough of the case to allow the judge reading the notice of motion to understand why the relief should be granted. Brevity is important, as judges will not have the time to review a notice of motion unless it is short, but a mere recitation of statutory or regulatory provisions and a

---

[8]   *I.e.*, "such further and other relief", *etc.*

legal conclusion tells the court virtually nothing, is unhelpful, and is not convincing.

At a minimum the grounds ought to include:

1.   A paragraph about the parties and the case;
2.   Why, in the instant case, the relief is being sought; and
3.   Relevant statutory or regulatory provisions.

Contrast these two grounds in a motion for summary judgment:

A

1.   *There is no genuine issue for trial;*

2.   *Rules [Relevant rules allowing this court to hear the motion and deal with motions for judgment]; and*

3.   *Such further and other grounds as counsel may advise and this court accept.*

or

B

1.   *The plaintiff has sued the defendant for monies due, but not paid, on a promissory note;*

2.   *The defendant has pleaded various defences, but none of them raises any genuine issue for trial;*

3.   *Rules [Relevant rules allowing this court to hear the motion and deal with motions for judgment]; and*

4.   *Such further and other grounds as counsel may advise and this court accept.*

Ground *B* is somewhat longer than ground *A*, but ground *B* actually conveys relevant information to the court and allows the judge to know what to look for when reviewing the rest of the motion materials.

As a matter of law, the grounds for the motion need to give a sufficient basis for the motion to be granted. Some legal analysis ought to go into the grounds — if you cannot justify the granting of the relief sought, you ought to reconsider the motion. Everything needed to justify the relief should be in the grounds, although no reference to the evidence whereby proof of the grounds is to be made should appear. Spending time on the grounds leads to a more convincing notice of motion and also provides a blueprint for whatever evidence will be put forward to support the motion — once you know what has to be proven, it becomes easier to set out the necessary proof.

APPLICATIONS

Generally, litigation is conducted by action with exchanges of pleadings, discovery, and trial by *viva voce* evidence. That said, where prescribed by statute or where factual disputes are likely to be limited, it is possible to proceed by application rather than by action. An application resembles a motion in structure; albeit a motion that finally determines the dispute between the parties.

Specifically, an application is commenced by the issuance of a notice of application, which is served together with supporting material, and forms the basis of the proceeding. The notice of application is a combination of a statement of claim and a notice of motion.

A notice of application contains a customary warning, as prescribed by the relevant rules of practice, which is followed by a description of a precise relief sought, the grounds for that relief and the evidence to be used in support of the application. An application, unlike a motion, must always be brought before a judge, thus there is no problem of deciding to which level of court to apply. Some care is needed as to where the application is brought. Often the statutes allowing applications have geographic jurisdictional restrictions on where an application can be heard. The remaining parts of the notice of application are completed as a notice of motion.

In drafting application materials, the risk of a court-ordered trial should not be overlooked. Where a judge sees real issues of credibility, the judge can — and will — convert the application into an action.[9] Since converting an application into an action will result in enormous expense and inconvenience, great care should be taken to show that, while issues of law may be in dispute, no significant factual issues are in question. In effect, the same considerations arising in a motion for summary judgment also apply in applications.

EVIDENCE TO BE RELIED ON

NO AFFIDAVIT

In some cases[10] no evidence can be used in support of a motion or application. Such cases, however, are extraordinary and are far from the norm. Most of the time motions and applications are supported by affidavit evidence.

As a matter of written advocacy, an affidavit is very helpful. It allows a selection of relevant material to be placed in the context of litigation

---

[9] For example, *Renegade Capital Corp. v. Hees International Bancorp Ltd.* (1990), 73 O.R. (2d) 311 (H.C.J.); *Island of Bob-Lo Co. v. Malden (Township)*, [1969] 2 O.R. 535 (C.A.).

[10] Generally, civil pleadings motions: See, for example, the Ontario Rules of Civil Procedure, R.R.O. 1990, Reg. 194, R. 21 or the Federal Court Rules, 1998, Rr. 213-219.

and put before the court. An affidavit allows your clients to tell their story, in their words, in a form structured by you. Nevertheless, an affidavit is not always necessary. Other evidence — transcripts of discovery, examinations of witnesses on a pending motion, requests to admit, and the like — can support a motion or application. On occasion, particularly if cross-examination of the witnesses on their affidavit will lead to great delay or allow the other side to muddy the waters by raising extraneous matters, it is best to proceed without an affidavit. If this is the case, even more care in setting out the grounds for the relief in the notice of motion must be taken. The function of the affidavit in telling a story is lost and the story must then be told by the notice of motion.

AFFIDAVIT

At the outset, consider who can, or ought, to swear an affidavit. While information and belief is generally admissible on motions,[11] this sort of evidence is weak unless it deals with obviously non-contentious matters. Evidence on applications ought to come from deponents with personal knowledge. An affidavit is testimony and it ought to be confined to facts, and not contain speculation. Having the affiant expressly and obviously state how they know something (for example, "I saw", "I heard", *etc.*) adds to an affidavit's immediacy and persuasiveness. If it is impossible to have someone with direct knowledge give an affidavit, say so and explain why. This leads to the possibility that more than one affidavit may be necessary to support a motion. Multiple affidavits of several affiants make sense, but, in such case at least one affidavit ought to tell the entire story, while making explicit reference to what is said in other affidavits.

For example, consider a motion requiring some degree of expert evidence. The main affiant could simply say that he or she was advised, and believed, some fact told to him or her by an expert. Alternatively — and this is far more persuasive — the main affiant could say what he or she was told by the expert, and then could reference a brief affidavit of the expert stating, as personal knowledge, that fact.

At least one affidavit ought to outline the story and be the self-contained source of evidentary background for the motion. The main affidavit is self-contained and can be read alone. The subsidiary affidavits, by contrast, say little in themselves and cannot be read except in context of the main affidavit. Usually, but not always, such affidavit is best sworn by the party or, if the party is an artificial person, whoever is closest to the matter. Affidavits of secretaries or lawyers are frowned upon except for purely procedural matters that can hardly be contested

---

[11]   See, for example, Ontario r. 39.01(4); but not, generally, on applications: See, for example, Ontario r. 39.01(5).

and are, in any event, not within a party's direct knowledge.[12] Judges do not like to make findings of credibility relating to counsel or their staff and it is better to avoid such issues entirely by allowing evidence to come from the parties and not their lawyers.

The story to be told by the main affidavit ought to be succinct; credibility will not be judged by number of pages. A judge, short on time to read the affidavit in full, wants the relevant facts and little more. While placement of the motion in the context of the litigation is necessary, only the briefest description is sufficient. Exhibits to affidavits, regardless of length, do not add a burden to the court's time, and many details can be put into the exhibits and left out of the affidavit.

An introductory paragraph about the litigation is always appropriate. The paragraph should be a fair, but brief, description of the case and its issues. It may be that much detail can be omitted by reference to the pleadings or notice of application. It is not necessary to outline what the motion is for in the introductory paragraph, although that will likely become evident from the rest of the affidavit; the notice of motion has set out what the motion is about. An appropriate introductory motion might be as follows:

> *As can be seen from the pleadings, true copies of which I attach as Exhibits "A", "B" and "C", I have sued my former doctor [defendant] for sexual assault. [Defendant] has admitted having intercourse with me but says I consented. The main issue in the case is consent, and whether it can apply in a doctor/patient relationship.*

This introduction, while brief, outlines the case and its issues in a neutral fashion. It does not take a great deal of the court's time, but gives the court the background of the case.

The remainder of the affidavit should deal with the substance of the motion or application. In some cases, say a motion for judgment, this is, in effect, a full review of the entire case. In other situations, say a demand for refusals and undertakings on an examination for discovery, very little more about the substance of the case is needed. Either way, the "grounds for relief sought" from the notice of motion ought to serve as a checklist of matters to prove by the affidavit. That said, the remainder of the affidavit is not merely a recitation of the grounds — rather, the affidavit must give a coherent account of events that show by testimony and exhibit the facts forming the grounds for relief sought.

For example, suppose a ground for relief sought is "demand for an affidavit of production has been made and ignored". A paragraph in the affidavit supporting that ground might be as follows:

> *After pleadings closed, my lawyer telephoned the defendant's lawyer. My lawyer spoke to [whoever] on [whenever] and asked for the defendant's productions. Two weeks went by and the defendant did not deliver anything, so I*

---

[12] For example, motions based on delivery of materials, such as a requirement that an affidavit of documents or production be made since pleadings are closed.

told my lawyer to write and request the affidavit of production. That letter was sent, and I attach a copy as Exhibit "A". No response, written or verbal, to the letter has been received.

The ground is clearly established by the affidavit.

If the affidavit is short (under four pages), it is unnecessary to include headings in the document. For longer affidavits, however, clear, brief headings make the affidavit easier to use and follow. The headings ought to be neutral but informative. Thus, headings such as "Issues Arise As Product Fails" are useful whereas headings such as "Events After March 27, 1997" are not. Similarly, a heading "Contract Breached", while stating a position, is helpful but the heading "Flagrant and Willful Breach of Contract" is insulting to the court and unpersuasive.

Raising Improper Conduct

Where something is improper in the party opposite's conduct, it may be helpful to raise that conduct. Assuming the conduct is not directly relevant to the motion, it ought to be dealt with carefully and not be made a main focus of the affidavit — such a focus will annoy the court and may lead to the motion being overlooked and the subsidiary improper conduct taking centerstage.

A good way to deal with the improper conduct is not to reference it at all in the notice of motion and to put it, under a neutral heading such as "Defendant's Procedural Noncompliance", at the end of the main affidavit. In that subsection, after all the matters necessary for the granting of the relief sought are dealt with, describe the improper conduct in factual, non-inflammatory paragraphs. Attach any relevant correspondence, certificates of non-attendance or other materials. Before closing this section, it is helpful to note explicitly that the improper conduct is raised only to put the motion in context. A closing paragraph might read as follows:

> *I have raised the difficulty I had getting the defendant to come to discovery because it shows the defendant's attitude to this litigation and not because it directly relates to whether the refusals made during discovery are proper. I do believe, however, that the difficulty in arranging discovery is relevant in that it shows an ongoing refusal of the defendant to follow the Rules and this is consistent with a refusal to answer proper questions on discovery.*

SAMPLE AFFIDAVIT

To illustrate some of these points relating to affidavits, a sample affidavit[13] follows.

---

[13] The authors thank their colleague and friend, Jack Hope, for this affidavit. It was modified by the authors and any infelicities are the authors' and not Mr. Hope's.

AFFIDAVIT

I, LISA JONES, of the City of Toronto, MAKE OATH AND SAY AS FOLLOWS:

1. The applicant and I were married to each other on the 30th day of September, 1986, in the City of Hamilton, in the Country of Bermuda, although we both were, at the time, Canadian residents and continue to be so.

2. The respondent and myself were separated on or about November 3rd, 1993 and were divorced pursuant to a judgment of the Honourable Justice Patel on April 22, 1996. A certificate of divorce was duly obtained and in fact, the respondent has since remarried.

3. There is one child of the marriage, Sally Jones, born the 8th day of July, 1990 ("Sally").

4. The aforesaid judgment for divorce was an uncontested proceeding and dealt with the dissolution of the marriage only as all ancillary issues had been dealt with by way of a separation agreement dated the 18th day of August, 1994, which agreement was negotiated with the benefit of independent counsel for both parties.

5. This is an application to vary the custody and access provisions of the separation agreement, which are set out in paragraph 5 thereof, and which agreement is attached as Exhibit "A" to this my affidavit.

6. Paragraph 5 provides for joint custody of the child and further provides that the child will have her primary residence with the applicant wife and that the wife will have the day-to-day care and control of the child (paragraph 5.1).

7. The agreement further provides that the child will attend at the day care centre and/or school located closest to the wife's home (paragraph 5.2).

8. The agreement further provides that the husband will have liberal and general access to the child on a series of specified times including one day each weekend, two sleep-over days each week, and various holiday provisions as more particularly set out in paragraph 5.3 of the said agreement.

9. The agreement further provides that, in the event of a dispute, the parties will seek mediation prior to seeking relief from a court (paragraph 5.9).

10. Joint custody is no longer in the best interest of Sally. The respondent, especially since his re-marriage in or about October 1997, has refused to communicate with me in respect of Sally, or any other matter, insisting that all our communication be by way of letter or voicemail only. He has also taken many unilateral acts without consulting with me,

such as removing Sally from her school and enrolling her in a Catholic school on two separate occasions. He further refuses to consent to psychological counselling for Sally, who appears to be suffering from the growing tension between the respondent and myself. These and other events are further particularized below.

11. Although relations between the respondent and myself have always been strained, I did my best to cooperate with the joint custodial regime I had agreed to in the separation agreement referred to above. After the respondent's remarriage in or about October 1997, however, to a woman with two children of her own only slightly older than Sally, the difficulties began to increase significantly. In or about that month, after an access weekend, I discovered that the respondent had enrolled my daughter in a Catholic school near his home without any consultation or warning. This was, of course, in direct contravention of paragraph 5.2 of our separation agreement but, even more significantly, represents an attitude of unilateral action and disrespect, if not contempt, for my involvement in the raising of Sally that has now come to characterize our relationship.

12. I returned Sally to the school she had regularly attended near my home. In or about April of 1998 the respondent again enrolled Sally in the same Catholic school without consultation or warning. This time I again returned her to her usual school and wrote a letter to the guidance counsellor indicating that, according to the terms of the separation agreement, no fundamental changes were to take place without the written consent of both custodial parents. A copy of this letter was sent both to the principal of the Sally's regular school, Cord Public School, and to the principal of St. Patrick's Catholic School, the school in which her father had now twice enrolled Sally. A copy of this letter is attached hereto and marked as Exhibit "B" to this my affidavit.

13. A meeting was arranged at Cord Public School in order to discuss these problems and, more importantly, in order to discuss counselling for Sally. This meeting was scheduled for June 3rd, 1998. An argument developed between the respondent and myself as to whether his new wife, Ann Smith, would be attending this meeting. It was my feeling that the school meeting would be more productive in the presence of only Sally and her father and mother. As a result of my refusal to permit his new wife to attend the meeting, the respondent sent me a letter on May 27th, 1998 stating that:

- *All phone calls at my place of work will end immediately.*
- *Information relating to significant daily management details regarding Sally will be voicemailed.*
- *All further communications regarding Sally will be done by letter.*
- *Re: Wednesday, June 3rd, 1998*
  Meeting: 9:00 a.m.
  Secord School
  1) Meeting cancelled.

A copy of this letter is set out as Exhibit "C" to this my affidavit.

14. The respondent has, since that date, insisted on a routine of contact by letter and voicemail only. For instance, on June 2nd, 1998, he left a note in the following terms:

> *Due to preplanned events, I will pick up Sally from school at 3:45 p.m., on Friday, June 5. If this creates a problem, contact me by voicemail.*
>
> *Re birthday party: Please send a note with Sally to let me know your antici-pated pick up and drop off times on Saturday so that we can schedule our day. [signature] "A. Jones"*

Attached hereto and marked as Exhibit "D" to this my affidavit is a true copy of this letter.

15. Somewhat later that same year, the respondent, in the belief that I was making plans to change Sally's school, sent me a letter in the mandatory style that had now come to characterize all his communica-tions, reminding me that there is a joint custodial agreement in place and that any proposed changes must be communicated to him for his approval. He further went on to criticize my letter of May 20th, 1998, for attempting to exclude his current wife from any discussions regarding Sally and further complained that this letter had been placed in Sally's O.S.R. (school file). His letter contained the following comments:

> *As Ms. Smith is now legally Sally's stepmother, this information can be discussed with her. You are hereby instructed to remove this letter from the O.S.R. Should you fail to do so, I have been advised that I can have this document removed by court order.*
> *You are further instructed to stop any further non-written communication with me unless it is an EMERGENCY directly affecting Sally.*
> *I have communicated with the school and notified them that any corre-spondence regarding Sally should be sent directly to me by mail or with Sally. Under no circumstances, is this information to be transmitted by my ex-wife. "A. Jones".*

Attached hereto and marked as Exhibit "E" to this my affidavit is a true copy of this letter.

16. The respondent has taken his refusal to communicate with me to unreasonable extremes. For instance, during an access weekend last August, Sally developed pneumonia on the Saturday morning while she was with the respondent and his family. Instead of keeping me informed as to her progress, they simply left me a telephone message on Sunday night stating that Sally had developed pneumonia and that they would call me. I attempted to telephone them all night and left messages throughout the night but they would not answer their phone nor return my messages until the next morning when, once again, I was simply left with a telephone message that Sally would not be returning that day due to her illness. I can interpret this only as a deliberate and vindictive attempt to create undue stress and aggravation for me. The respondent is

aware that I do not drive and could not simply come to their house to obtain further information, nor would I have been permitted there, given the state of affairs between us.

17. The current access schedule has changed somewhat since the original separation agreement. Sally now spends alternate weekends with her father and sleeps over at his home on Tuesday and Wednesday nights each week. These periods of access have become highly stressful for Sally. I can only assume this is due to, among other things, the deteriorating relationship between the respondent and myself and the manner in which these difficulties are made manifest during Sally's visits. For instance, I am not permitted to telephone their home to talk to Sally and can only leave voicemail messages. While Sally is permitted to call me at times, her calls appear to be screened as she appears stilted and inhibited on the telephone as if she is watching every word.

18. It is my understanding from Sally that the respondent's wife, Ann Smith, is also a source of significant emotional pressure. Sally has told me that Ann Smith, on occasion, has stated that my expressions of love for Sally are false.

19. Sally has also advised me that she has been subject to punishment in their household for confiding in me. For instance, Sally advises that she was once accused of lying about whether or not she sucked her thumb at my home. While Sally maintained that she didn't, after extended questioning she eventually "confessed" in order to end the episode. She then told me about this incident and I communicated to the respondent and his wife that Sally did not in fact suck her thumb. She was then punished for both lying and "disrespecting" their household by telling the story to me. She was made to write a letter to the whole family confessing to character faults and promising to change. (Sally was then an 8-year-old child.) Since this incident, Sally has apparently earned the label of "liar" in the respondent's household and is frequently called by this term. I cannot verify this as her father refuses to speak to me.

20. Sally advises me that she always feels that she is "in trouble" at the respondent's home and that this feeling is furthered by the two children of Ann Smith, who are approximately two years older than she. One of them, for instance, will initiate conversations with Sally whereby she is asked to admit that it would not really matter if her mother died.

21. Sally advised that she has also been subjected to spanking on her buttocks by Ann Smith. Once again, while confiding in me the humiliation she felt at being spanked by this woman who was not her mother, she expressed fear that if this story ever got back to her father or his wife, she would be punished further for failing to keep it a secret.

22. Based on my experience with the respondent, it is my opinion that he does not deal well with emotional distress himself and I am concerned that he may not be able to recognize it in Sally or her need for counsel-

ling. Therefore, I strongly feel the need to consult a third party for assessment and possible mediation on Sally's behalf.

23. It is my belief that Sally has suffered significant psychological and emotional stresses as a result of this ongoing dispute and that she would benefit from counselling. For example, just prior to her school concert last November 17, 1998, Sally told me that she'd like to be hit by a truck, that her life is too complicated and that she hates her life. She was sobbing deeply and revealed to me profound and serious unhappiness. I am unable to discuss this with her father or properly communicate her state to him as he simply refuses to talk to me. This type of discussion cannot be conducted by letter or voicemail. I have attempted to seek the permission of the respondent for psychological counselling, but he has steadfastly refused to permit it. I recently had my lawyer, Jack W. Hope, write to the respondent requesting permission for Sally to see a Dr. Judy Doe in order to pursue counselling. The respondent replied by letter stating that

Permission for psychological counselling with Dr. Judy Doe will not be forthcoming.

A copy of this letter is set out as Exhibit "F" to this my affidavit.

24. In accordance with our separation agreement, I had my lawyer, Jack W. Hope, suggest to the respondent that we pursue mediation of our dispute in order to explore a resolution without court proceedings. His reply was as follows:

In response to your letter of December 9th, 1998, I have carefully read and considered all the statements that it contains. Therefore, I feel that the only viable option, in the best interest of Sally, is an expedient and a definitive decision that can be provided by a court of law.

A copy of this letter (dated December 10th, 1998) is set out as Exhibit "G" to this my affidavit.

25. Recently on March 22, 1998, before taking Sally to school, she told me, in a very serious tone, that we would have to have a conversation about all the "lies" my lawyer is writing about her. I do not wish to involve Sally, who is only eight years old, so directly in these proceedings. I feel that any attempt I make to convey my concerns to her father is inappropriately communicated to Sally, which only compounds the problem and makes her feel responsible.

26. In light of the difficulties set out above, it is my belief that it would be in Sally's best interest if I were to be the sole custodial parent. She continues to attend school near my house and all her friends from school live in our area. Joint custody has clearly broken down irretrievably and I accordingly seek an Order for sole custody from this court until and unless there is change in the respondent's willingness to communicate with me in respect of Sally's interests.

27. I would also seek an Order amending access such that:

   (a) Sally would spend every alternate weekend with her father, from Friday evening to Monday morning;

   (b) Sally would spend additional time with her father during holidays and, in particular, a six-week period every summer, commencing July 9th.

28. This schedule would avoid the disruption of mid-week sleepovers. The extended summer holiday would also coincide with the fact that the respondent, as a teacher, also has his summer off. I would, of course, continue to be flexible with respect to access and not limit Sally or her father to a rigid schedule.

Chapter 6

PRE-TRIAL CONFERENCE MEMORANDA

INTRODUCTION

Both criminal and civil cases have pre-trial hearings. The purpose of these hearings is "to consider the matters that, to promote a fair and expeditious hearing, would be better decided before the start of the proceedings".[1] Which is a fancy way of saying "Let's look at the issues and evidence in this case to see if it can't be settled without a trial".

As we've mentioned earlier, today's justice system is filled to overflowing with cases. Keeping 99 per cent of them out of court isn't just a good idea — it's a necessity. This is why the criminal and civil systems have built in a lot of barriers to stop the parties from having a trial. Pre-trial hearings (or "pre-trials" for short) are a very powerful device.

Practically speaking, two types of issues are considered at a pre-trial. First, scheduling and procedural matters can be dealt with at this time, often leading to orders as to the date and order of trial, further disclosure obligations, and the like. Second, and perhaps more important, judges almost invariably attempt to promote settlement at the pre-trial.

Civil pre-trials, much more than their criminal counterparts, have a body and style of legal writing connected to them. Although this chapter deals with civil pre-trials specifically, the techniques outlined will apply, in most cases, to pre-trial memorandums as well. The rules of a pre-trial are simple: Each side meets with a judge (usually in chambers) and presents the merits of their case. There is no jury to impress, no devastating cross-examination, no shocking exhibits on display. It's "just the facts, ma'am", a chance to expose the merits of your case in all its glory — or all its weakness. As a general rule, the judge conducting the pre-trial will not conduct the trial and, except for orders emerging from the pre-trial, nothing that takes place at the pre-trial is disclosed outside the pre-trial. In effect, a pre-trial is a free test run of your case in front of a trained and experienced judicial officer. As a bonus, when the pre-trial is over, the judicial officer will give you a free ruling on what her or his verdict would have been. A pre-trial can be a real eye-opener for one or both sides in an intensely fought lawsuit, because there's a natural

---

[1]   *Criminal Code*, R.S.C. 1985, c. C-46, s. 625.1(1).

human tendency to focus only on a version of reality that belongs to you. It sometimes takes a jolt from a pre-trial judge to open a litigant's eyes about the true strengths and weaknesses of a case and to move the parties toward a settlement.

Don't think, however, that pre-trial judges give their assessments like robots. They are as human as the rest of us and, like most humans, they are subject to persuasion in an argument. Carry that a step further and you'll realize that if you can persuade a pre-trial judge that your case is particularly meritorious, the judge will probably advise the parties that, had the matter been in trial in front of her or him, she or he would have given judgment in favour of you. Imagine the fun you'll have walking into settlement negotiations armed with a pre-trial verdict like that.

To help the pre-trial judge see things your way, it's important to come to pre-trial with the fruits of good written advocacy — a convincing pre-trial memorandum that can lead a judge to urge settlement on terms favourable to you is a very valuable asset.

Even if you know that your opponent is so stubborn that a settlement is all but impossible, preparing a detailed pre-trial memorandum is worth the work. Writing out a concise version of your argument is the very best preparation for trial.

JUDGES AND PRE-TRIALS

Although it varies from jurisdiction to jurisdiction, judges seldom have a lot of time to prepare for pre-trial conferences. Usually, a judge will be given the written materials for several pre-trial conferences shortly before the conferences are scheduled. The judge will have only enough time to scan the materials quickly. As a result, when you're constructing your pre-trial memoranda, brevity and clarity are essential. Put yourself in the judge's shoes: Faced with a lengthy complex memorandum from one side and a concise, simple memorandum from the other side, wouldn't there be a powerful temptation to glance at the lengthy memorandum and read the concise memorandum closely? Similarly, if you were confronted with a flood of materials to read, the temptation to "pigeon-hole" the case, without giving it careful consideration, would be strong.

If a pre-trial conference is to be effective, the memorandum must be short and quickly direct the judge to the real issues in the case. That said, brevity can go too far; your memorandum must not be superficial. Good legal writing must focus on the issues that really are before the court, succinctly but with substance. What's your model for this level of communication? An effective technique for choosing only the necessary material for the pre-trial memorandum is to imagine what you would tell another lawyer about the case during a recess. If your friend is like most lawyers, she has a case that she's dying to describe to you. In that circumstance, you want to give just enough facts to receive an honest, but quick, appraisal from your friend. That's just the sort of bare-bones description that the pre-trial judge needs.

CONTENT IN PRE-TRIAL MEMORANDA

Some jurisdictions are writer-friendly and have few prescribed formats for a pre-trial memorandum. Other jurisdictions make the format rigid and leave room for no creativity at all. Regardless of format require-ments, there are certain matters that must be included in any pre-trial memorandum.

Since a major purpose of the pre-trial is scheduling, you should come with an estimate of the anticipated length of trial. You should also be ready to state who counsel will be at trial, the number of witnesses, and any times the trial cannot be heard. Be realistic in anticipating your trial's length. An otherwise persuasive memorandum with a preposterous anticipated trial length downgrades the credibility of your whole case. A judge will not have faith in a lawyer who says that a partnership breakup trial will be done in a day and a half.

Beyond such bread-and-butter issues, a pre-trial memorandum should also deal, in an honest and straightforward way, with the merits of the case itself, and also advance a reasonable settlement.[2] Focus on the real merits of the case. If your statement of defence sets out four defences, and one of them works much better than the others, focus your materials on that defence. Remember: The judge's time is limited — use your time wisely.

PARTY'S POSITION

Remember: The importance of the pre-trial memorandum is to convince the court of the strength of your position. The word "convince" is important — a pre-trial memorandum that is a mere rehashing of the pleading is of no use at all. Instead, you've got to offer a concise yet detailed position statement, with references to evidence, focusing on the issues in the case. The name for this first portion of a pre-trial memoran-dum is entitled "Party's Position".

It is helpful to begin the "Party's Position" section with a brief intro-duction outlining, in a sentence or two, what type of case is before the court. You should also explicitly state that, to aid possible settlement, the pre-trial memorandum will detail evidence more fully than usual in such a document. Of course, you will remember that this introduction is not a

---

[2] If criminal conduct is dealt with, either in a criminal or civil pre-trial memorandum, no direct admission should be made. Rather, it is preferable to adopt an oblique phrasing to avoid, even in the context of pre-trial, an admission that may be problematic later. The phrase, "assuming, for the purposes of this pre-trial, that the allegations of [what-ever] are true" is very helpful.

licence to ramble on. You will lose the judicial reader unless you stick to relevant matters. Here's an example of a good introduction:

> *The plaintiff claims for wrongful dismissal and the defendant says there was cause for dismissal. This pre-trial memorandum outlines the plaintiff's case in more detail than is customary because the plaintiff believes such detail may promote settlement.*

The section following this introduction will set out the legal/factual issues in dispute. Do not gloss over issues, but, at the same time, do not give so much detail that the court may lose interest. A good rule is to confine the party's position to not more than four issues. In the wrongful dismissal case we looked at a moment ago, the issues might be:

1. *Was there cause to dismiss the plaintiff?*

2. *If not, how long was the plaintiff's service and what was appropriate severance?*

Notice that we avoid "issues" that are non-issues, such as "Was the plaintiff dismissed?" or "Was the plaintiff employed?". You have to prove those details at trial, but they can just be assumed at pre-trial.

Notice also that we avoided framing the remaining issues in anything but a neutral fashion. It sounds good to ask a jury "Did the heartless defendant dismiss the plaintiff after 20 years of back-breaking toil in his sweatshop?", but inflammatory phrasing will neither impress nor persuade the court.

The list of issues can be used as subheadings for your recital of the party's position. Each subsection ought to be fairly short, two or three pages at most, but direct references to evidence and law are appropriate. The purpose of such references is to persuade the court that you have a good case, not to overwhelm the court, or even to convince the court that your case is unanswerable. For this reason, a detailed legal analysis is not appropriate; at most, make brief case law extracts and nothing more.

For the same reason, lengthy transcript excerpts are not needed. More effective are: (a) summary statements of trends in case law; and (b) admissions or assertions made in discovery, together with references to the cases or transcripts. Combining case law and transcript excerpts in the pre-trial memorandum is helpful, because it allows the judge to look at the cases or transcripts if you've aroused their curiosity.

Choice of language is important when you're setting out the party's position. Short, clear sentences convey information more forcefully than longer, more complex, sentences. Today's trend is for the plaintiff to use more concrete language, while the defendant will usually do better to use abstract language. Short sentences present information emphatically and are good vehicles for helpful information. Consider the following ways of conveying the same information:

A

Danny shot his father John twice. Danny used a sawed-off shotgun. Danny said he was angry because of his grandfather's will.

or

B

The defendant was upset over the probating of his grandfather's will and, as a result, became embroiled in a dispute with the plaintiff, his father, which led to the plaintiff being shot with a shotgun altered so as to be a prohibited weapon.

The information conveyed in *A* and *B* is the same, but there is far less emphasis on the bare facts in *B*. If you're the party suing Danny, you'll use *A*. As Danny's defence counsel, you'll want to use *B*.

By the way, no case is perfect, and the pre-trial judge knows this. It's likely that, somewhere along the line, your clients did something that you sure wish they hadn't. Should you skip over your clients' *faux pas* in your pre-trial memorandum? Usually, no. It is better to disclose harmful information before your opponent does. Use non-specific, general and impersonal language.

When you have to admit to something unfavourable, spell out the negative information following positive information. This tends to weaken the impact of the negative. Word order is important here. Consider these two descriptions:

A

Danny is a loving father and a skilled machinist, who has a criminal record and a drug abuse problem.

or

B

Danny has a criminal record and a drug abuse problem, but is a loving father and a skilled machinist.

The first sentence conveys an image of a good man with issues; the second sentence pictures a criminal with, perhaps, a few redeeming qualities.

WHAT EVERY PRE-TRIAL MEMORANDUM SHOULD CONTAIN

Here's a brief list of headings which should go into your pre-trial memorandum. There is no set order for these headings; put them in whatever order makes the most sense with the case you've got.

- Short style of cause
- Trial date
- Pre-trial date
- Counsel at trial (list counsel for all parties)
- Brief summary of the claim
- Brief summary of the defence (especially important if you represent the defendant)
- Issues outstanding
- Discussion of the issues
- Quantum of damages (or sentencing considerations, if this is a criminal matter)
- Witnesses anticipated at trial
- Documents and requests to admit
- Estimated length of trial [3]
- Settlement prospects

A SAMPLE PRE-TRIAL MEMORANDUM

We've given you bits and pieces of pre-trial memoranda up to this point. Now, these suggestions will be illustrated in detail with a complete sample pre-trial memorandum. Obviously, as the lawyer, you will have to exercise your own good judgment to decide what is needed in your own case. Legal writing, like any writing you do, is an extension of you, and every lawyer has an individual writing style. The following sample is just one of hundreds of effective pre-trial memoranda that could be written for the same case. Having said this, though, keep a couple of points in mind:

- A plaintiff's pre-trial memorandum in something dry like a promissory note claim should not be very long or detailed in legal issues unless the defendant has raised a truly remarkable defence. By contrast, when asserting an unusual or novel position, more emphasis on law is appropriate and desirable.

---

[3] In today's age of overcrowded courtrooms, this is no small detail. Some years ago, a criminal trial began on a muggy day in July. Crown and defence had estimated the case would take one day, but cross-examination of the Crown's key witness turned into a marathon and, by 4:00 p.m., it was obvious that the trial wouldn't be completed that day. At the afternoon break, Crown and defence went to the trial coordinator's office and asked her to confer with the trial judge to see when in the future he and the courthouse were available to resume the trial. When both counsel returned to the courtroom, the judge announced the resumption date: January 8, six months in the future! He concluded that day's proceedings by announcing "May I be the first to wish counsel a Happy New Year".

When the case actually resumed, six months later, Crown and defence worked out a plea bargain, thanks in large part to the fact that a snowstorm prevented two key Crown witnesses from attending court!

- An unwritten question which is always found at the end of a pre-trial memorandum is "Well, that's our case, Your Honour. What do you think of it?" Everything else in the memorandum is a build-up to that question.
- Never forget that the primary purpose of a pre-trial memorandum is to enlist the help of the pre-trial judge to pressure the other side to agree to give your client a just and reasonable settlement. As one wag put it, trials are like amputations: They're exciting and a lot of fun for the practitioner doing them, but the clients certainly won't enjoy them.

This sample pre-trial memorandum outlines a civil action filed by a counselling patient seeking damages from her therapist, who took advantage of their relationship to coerce her into having sex with him.

PRE-TRIAL MEMORANDUM

Short Style of Cause	Jones v. Stone, *et al.*
Trial Date	Unknown, likely late 2001
Pre-Trial Date	October 22, 2000

Counsel at Trial

Party	*Represented By*
Katherine Jones	Barney C. Roubelle
Counselling Centre and Karen Doe	Paul Kary
Fred Stone	Self

(*n.b.*: Counsel have agreed to dismiss, without costs, the claim against Karen Doe and an order to that effect is sought at the pre-trial.)

Brief Summary of Claim

Katherine Jones (the "plaintiff") says that she sought grief counselling from the Counselling Centre (the "Centre"), in connection with the death of her son. Such counselling was provided by an employee and, eventually, director of the Centre, Fred Stone ("Stone"). During the course of the counselling, Stone, in breach of his obligations as a counsellor, engaged in sexual relations with the plaintiff. The relations were degrading and, because of the relationship between the parties, could not be legally consented to by the plaintiff. These relations continued over a lengthy period having the result of (1) denying the plaintiff proper, or any, counselling and (2) causing significant and long-term psychiatric harm to the plaintiff. The Centre is liable for the delict of Stone as Stone's principal and also for a failure to supervise and ensure proper counselling therapy was given.

Issues Outstanding

1. *Liability of Stone*

2. *Liability of the Centre*

3. *Quantum of Damages*

Discussion of Issues

1. Liability of Stone

During examinations Stone acknowledged the sexual conduct, including incidents relating to bondage and degradation (q 1030ff). Stone hit the plaintiff with his hand or a belt during counselling sessions (q 1632-1035). Stone further acknowledged the conduct largely accrued during scheduled counselling sessions (q 947) and involved activity which customarily would be taken as being for his sexual pleasure as opposed to that of the plaintiff. Finally, Stone acknowledged being aware at the time of the relations that it was contrary to accepted opinion for counsellors to have sexual relations with patients (q 1000).

It is also relevant, perhaps, that Stone tried to cover up the sexual conduct once the plaintiff decided to disclose it (q 1064).

The Centre had no material evidence, one way or another, regarding the sexual incidents.

The evidence of the plaintiff is that the sexual incidents took place as an integral part of the counselling and that Stone used his authority to schedule the locations and circumstances of counselling sessions to ensure he obtained sexual gratification (see Tab 1). The plaintiff's evidence is she needed counselling, felt powerless compared to Stone and deeply ashamed by what happened, but was unable to change the situation (see Tab 2).

Two cases are especially helpful here, *Norberg v. Wynrib* (1992), 92 D.L.R. (4th) 449 (S.C.C.) (Tab 3) and *C. (N.) v. Blank*, [1998] O.J. 2544 (Gen. Div.) (Tab 4) [a fictitious case].

In *Norberg* a physician prescribed drugs to a drug-addicted patient in return for sexual favours. The patient sued for battery and the defendant raised a defence of consent. In a judgment that was unanimous as to liability the court held that, in view of the inequality of power between the parties and the exploitative nature of the relationship, consent was not an available defence. The court referred, with approval, to P. Coleman, "Sex in Power Dependency Relationships" 53 Albany L. Rev. 95, 96-97, commenting:

The common element in power dependency relationships is an underlying personal or professional association which creates a significant power imbalance between the parties… Exploitation occurs when the "powerful" person abuses the position of authority by inducing the "dependent" person into a sexual relationship, thereby causing harm [p. 463].

The court explicitly refers to "psychotherapist-patient, physician-patient" as examples of over-dependent relations (p. 463).

The *Blank* decision, which is compared to the present case in detail in Tab 5, dealt with a psychologist who engaged in sexual relations with a patient. In granting damages totalling $356,275.98 (including a $30,000 FLA claim), Justice Aitken commented, at para. 173ff:

[Fictitious case law quotation omitted.]

The present case stands on four squares with *Norberg* and *Blank*. As set out in further detail in Tab 5, the relationship between Stone and the plaintiff was based on a power imbalance, was exploitive and arose from a breach of duty as a counsellor.

In this regard, the reports of Peter Jody, Ph.D., C.Psych (Tab 6) and A.F.J. Bell, MB, BS, BHA, DPM, MRC Psych, FRANECP (Tab 7) are illuminating. The extent of the exploitation is very clear from Dr. Jody's report at page 3, where he writes:

The abuse was intrusive and coercive in nature. It initially began by Mr. Stone instructing Ms. Jones to engage in acts such as sucking his nipples for "therapeutic" reasons. The abuse escalated to including fondling, spanking, forced exposure to pornography, fellatio, with the demand to ingest his semen. This abuse, which span for nearly two years and took place on a monthly basis, occurred in a climate of degradation and humiliation. Ms. Jones was forced to perform oral sex while in a position of powerlessness. Other degrading acts included having to kiss Mr. Stone's anus and place his testicles in her mouth. Further, Mr. Stone showed no regard for Ms. Jones, to the degree that while bedridden after her hysterectomy, Mr. Stone compelled her to perform oral sex. Beyond having to deal with the physical nature of the assaults, Ms. Jones had to cope with the reality that this abuse was being perpetrated by a person in a position of trust and authority, her therapist.

2. Liability of the Centre

The wrongful acts of Stone took place during, and as part of, grief therapy offered by the Centre. Stone was hired by the Centre to act as a counsellor although it appears he had no academic training relevant to mental health work (although it is acknowledged he obtained limited on the job training after being hired). Stone rose to the position of director at the Centre in spite of knowledge by an employee of the Centre that, prior to even meeting the plaintiff, but while a counsellor he "stalked" at least two of his patients. Little, if any, meaningful supervision or review of Stone's work was made by the Centre.

It is submitted the Centre is liable as principal for Stone's acts and, regardless, for failing in its duty to ensure its patients were receiving appropriate and proper treatment. Indeed, the Centre appears to have taken no steps to ensure the quality of treatment was appropriate.

3. Quantum of Damages

The report of Luke Walker, C.A. (Tab 8) suggests damages for loss of income are between approximately $400,000 and $850,000. The plaintiff is a qualified professional nurse who has, in effect, been deprived of her livelihood by the defendants' delicts. Dr. Jody's report suggests the cost of necessary future care is in the range of $100,000 to $150,000 over a 20-year period. Actual expenses to date, including therapy, are in the range of $20,000.

Non-pecuniary general damages inclusive of aggravated damages are sizeable and, using the *Blank* decision as a guide, run in the range of $100,000. In this regard, the comment of the Supreme Court of Canada in *Andrews v. Grand & Toy Alberta Ltd.*, [1978] 1 W.W.R. 577 at 602 is helpful:

> There is no medium of exchange for happiness … The monetary evaluation of non-pecuniary losses is a philosophical and policy exercise more than a legal or logical one. The award must be fair and reasonable, fairness being gauged by earlier decisions; but the award must also of necessity be arbitrary or conventional. No money can provide true restitution.

Similarly, a sizeable award of punitive damages, perhaps in the range of $25,000 (*Blank*, para. 159) is appropriate. The comments of the court in *C. v. M.* (1990), 74 D.L.R. (4th) 129 at 136 (Ont. Gen. Div.), citing *Vorvis v. I.C.B.C.* (1989) 58 D.L.R. (4th) 193 at 201-02 (S.C.C.), are helpful:

> Punitive damages, as the name would indicate, are designed to punish. In this, they constitute an exception to the general common law rule that damages are designed to compensate the injured, not to punish the wrongdoer. Aggravated damages will frequently cover conduct which could also be the subject of punitive damages but the role of aggravated damages remains compensatory.

Accordingly, judgment, exclusive of interest and costs in the range of $500,000 to $1,000,000 would seem appropriate.

Witnesses

The plaintiff anticipates calling three experts, whose reports are attached, and who will be testifying personally. The plaintiff may call her husband to outline the current and continuing difficulties the plaintiff suffers.

The plaintiff is being examined by a medical doctor selected by the Centre. It is unclear if that doctor will testify.

Whether Stone will testify or participate fully at trial is unclear.

Documents and Requests to Admit

Requests to admit and document briefs have not been exchanged. It is not anticipated that documentary issues will be significant at trial.

Length of Trial

The plaintiff anticipates trial will last five to seven days although Stone's participation at trial may affect this.

Settlement

The plaintiff has prepared a more elaborate pre-trial conference memorandum than customary in the hope that settlement is possible.

Discussions between the Centre and the plaintiff have occurred, although the range of settlement proposed by the Centre is not acceptable. The plaintiff would be prepared to settle for an immediate all-inclusive payment of $485,000; however, no reduction from that figure will be accepted.

No settlement discussion with Stone has occurred between the plaintiff and Stone. Stone asserts he is unemployed and has been so for a lengthy period. The plaintiff suspects Stone has some assets, perhaps held in trust for Stone, which could be levied against. Apparently Stone had real estate while employed by the Centre.

All of which is respectfully submitted,

BARNEY C. ROUBELLE, counsel for the plaintiff

The pre-trial memorandum will always be a key piece of legal writing during your legal career. Master it, and you will have an important advantage at precisely the point in the case when it will be to your greatest advantage.

Chapter 7

ADR Briefs

ALTERNATIVE DISPUTE RESOLUTION

Alternative dispute resolution is still a fairly new concept in Canada and its form is still evolving. The principle behind ADR (that's the acronym for alternative dispute resolution) is simple: Litigation is gut-wrenching, time-consuming, and is prohibitively expensive for anyone except the rich or corporations. Emotionally, litigation is also unsatisfying because, once a trial has begun, the outcome is beyond the control of the parties and in the hands of strangers who don't know them at all.

ADR presents itself as an answer to all three of the negative practicalities of litigation. As a participatory activity, the litigants feel that they can control the process, which in turn can often lead to a quick resolution of a problem that formerly seemed irresolvable. Cost-wise, ADR is considerably less expensive than a trial, since it's faster and requires no trial preparation. Finally, it often works especially well because the end product has come about through the input and ideas of the parties involved; not through someone else's conception of what is right — which, if you ask many litigants post-trial, is all wrong.

FORMS OF ADR

The three most common ADR processes are negotiation, mediation and arbitration. Negotiation is well known and needs little elaboration. Confrontation — in the guise of two lawyers trying to come to a suitable resolution — is its most salient feature.

Mediation and arbitration are less well known, perhaps because they're less glamourous. Each features an outside third party, called (respectively) the mediator or arbitrator. Unlike the head-to-head confrontation of negotiation, mediation and arbitration are played out before someone neutral, whose role is to facilitate a resolution without the need to go to trial. To be sure, things can often get quite heated during mediation and arbitration, but having the neutral facilitator at the apex of the process gives it an entirely different dynamic.

Mediation, in a nutshell, amounts to assisted negotiation. In mediation, the parties are not bound to settle and the mediator, often called a third-party neutral, cannot impose settlement. The mediator is limited to focusing the parties on the issues that really divide them, encouraging compromise and, on occasion, pointing out to the parties the likely results of continuing to litigate. Since many mediators are retired judges, the impact of their views on continued litigation can be significant.

Arbitration is, in effect, allowing a jointly retained third party to decide a dispute as a judge. While the forms of arbitration, and appeal rights therefrom, vary, all arbitrations conclude with a determination of an issue put to the arbitrator. Arbitration has, quite properly, been called "Private Court".

Not surprisingly, mediation and arbitration have their own specialized paperwork, and that's what we'll be looking at in this chapter. In both mediation and arbitration, ADR briefs are prepared and submitted; however, the types of ADR briefs are very different in both form and content.

MEDIATION BRIEFS

It's important to keep several issues in mind when you're drafting mediation briefs. First, while mediation has a high success rate,[1] it is not always successful. If you bring out a previously unknown fact or source of information at mediation, and the mediation fails, its surprise value at trial is gone.[2] Second, mediation requires the parties to agree on the result. This means that your mediation brief needs to be directed toward fostering agreement; in other words, the "audience" of the mediation brief is the other side and the mediator, not the mediator alone.

During the mediation itself, the briefs are seldom referred to explicitly. Instead, the mediator often prefers to guide the parties directly to a possible settlement without focusing on the legal positions. Does this mean that you should lighten up on considerations of pure law in your brief? Not on your life! This apparent lack of use shouldn't distract you from your brief's importance. First, when you provide a fair and neutral factual background, the brief will form the basis for settlement negotiations. Second, the legal positions of the parties *are* useful, even if they might not be referred to a lot during the actual mediation. The relative strength or weakness of your legal position will always be there in the background, and it will affect the thought processes of all the parties, if only subconsciously, as the negotiations proceed.

---

[1] Ranging between 80 per cent and 85 per cent across Canada: J. Gross, "An Introduction to Alternative Dispute Resolution" (1995), 34:1 Alberta L. Rev. 5.

[2] Generally, mediations are taken to be confidential and admissions made cannot be used in subsequent litigation. Nevertheless, even if admissions cannot be used, the facts themselves, once revealed, are known to the parties. Similarly, once a "bottom line" settlement position is revealed, it can not be taken back.

What does a mediation brief look like? The actual form of mediation brief varies from mediator to mediator, but at a minimum, every brief ought to contain a neutral statement and chronology of the facts. Where facts are legitimately in dispute, you can make note of the disagreement and then highlight your side's version of the events. When disputes are merely positions and no real issue exists, then there will be no need to mention the varying positions.[3]

It is helpful, if not absolutely necessary, to give evidentiary references for the facts set out (*e.g.*, Discovery of Defendant, qq. 77-82). Such references add credibility to the facts asserted and allow quick reference to the evidence if necessary.

Beyond the statement of facts, mediation briefs ought to have a discussion of what issues arise from the facts. In this section, a brief legal discussion is appropriate. Care must be taken not to overextend the legal discussion so as to lose the mediator or the opposite counsel — the goal is to convince that there is a strong case and it is not necessary to do more than that.

Many mediation briefs finish with suggested settlements. In our opinion, this is a bad idea — the party opposite will probably do what you'd do in their shoes: mull over the proposals and find some serious fault with them. Remember, too, that the other side is likely to be suspicious of your proposals, simply because you're "the enemy". It is, generally, better not to give such proposals in advance. By all means suggest them during the mediation, but hold off until then, and keep them out of your mediation brief.

A SAMPLE MEDIATION BRIEF

Let's have a look at a typical mediation brief:

SUPERIOR COURT OF JUSTICE

MEDIATION MEMORANDUM OF KATHERINE JONES

Court File Number	1005/00
Short Title	Jones v. Stone *et al.*
Jury/Non-jury	Jury
Trial Date	Unknown, likely late 2001

---

[3]   For example, if a dispute exists as to what was said at a certain meeting, and witness recollections do vary, such dispute should be referenced. On the other hand, just because, say, a defendant's pleading denies delivery of goods that does not require reference if discovery clearly establishes delivery.

Parties and Counsel

Party	*Represented by*
Katherine Jones, accompanied by her husband	Barney C. Roubelle
Counselling Centre of Trout River, possibly accompanied by a representative of the insurer	Paul Kary
Fred Stone	Self

(*n.b.*: Stone is not attending the mediation and may not attend trial.)

Brief Summary of Case

Katherine Jones (the "plaintiff") sought grief counselling from the Counselling Centre (the "Centre"), in connection with the death of her son. Such counselling was provided by Fred Stone ("Stone"), an employee and, eventually, director of the Centre. During the course of the counselling, Stone, in breach of his obligations as a counsellor, engaged in sexual relations with the plaintiff. The relations were degrading and, because of the relationship between the parties, could not be legally consented to by the plaintiff. These relations continued over a lengthy period having the result of (1) denying the plaintiff proper, or any, counselling and (2) causing significant and long-term psychiatric harm to the plaintiff. The Centre is liable for the delict of Stone as Stone's principal and also for a failure to supervise and ensure proper counselling therapy was given.

Impact of Abuse on Plaintiff

Broadly put, the plaintiff, as a result of the abuse referred to above, says she became unable to work or function as a productive member of society for a lengthy period. She went to Stone as a qualified, working nurse suffering from grief due to the injury (and subsequent death) of her son. If Stone, and his employer, the Centre, had acted properly she would have gotten help for grief and moved on with life. In the event, her life was largely ruined for a lengthy and continuing period.

Issues Outstanding

1. Liability of Stone
2. Liability of the Centre
3. Quantum of damages

Discussion of Issues

1. Liability of Stone

During examinations Stone acknowledged the sexual conduct, including incidents relating to bondage and degradation (q 1030ff). Stone hit the plaintiff with his hand or a belt during counselling sessions (q 1632-1035). Stone further acknowledged the conduct largely accrued during scheduled counselling sessions (q 947) and involved activity which customarily would be taken as being for his sexual pleasure as opposed to that of the plaintiff. Finally, Stone acknowledged being aware at the time of the relations that it was contrary to accepted opinion for counsellors to have sexual relations with patients (q 1000).

It is also relevant, perhaps, that Stone tried to cover up the sexual conduct once the plaintiff decided to disclose it (q 1064).

The Centre had no material evidence, one way or another, regarding the sexual incidents.

The evidence of the plaintiff is that the sexual incidents took place as an integral part of the counselling and that Stone used his authority to schedule the locations and circumstances of counselling sessions to ensure he obtained sexual gratification (see Tab 1). The plaintiff's evidence is she needed counselling, felt powerless compared to Stone and deeply ashamed by what happened, but was unable to change the situation (see Tab 2).

Two cases are especially helpful here, *Norberg v. Wynrib* (1992), 92 D.L.R. (4th) 449 (S.C.C.) (Tab 3) and *C. (N.) v. Blank*, [1998] O.J. 2544 (O.C.J.) (Tab 4) [a fictitious case].

In *Norberg* a physician prescribed drugs to a drug addicted patient in return for sexual favours. The patient sued for battery and the defendant raised a defence of consent. In a judgment that was unanimous as to liability the court held that, in view of the inequality of power between the parties and the exploitative nature of the relationship, consent was not an available defence. The court referred, with approval, to P. Coleman, "Sex in Power Dependency Relationships" 53 Albany L. Rev. 95, 96-97, commenting:

> The common element in power dependency relationships is an underlying personal or professional association which creates a significant power imbalance between the parties... Exploitation occurs when the "powerful" person abuses the position of authority by inducing the "dependent" person into a sexual relationship, thereby causing harm [p. 463].

The court explicitly refers to "psychotherapist-patient, physician-patient" as examples of over dependent relations (p. 463).

The *Blank* decision, which is compared to the present case in detail in Tab 5, dealt with a psychologist who engaged in sexual relations with a patient. In granting damages totalling $356,275.98 (including a $30,000 FLA claim), Justice Aitken commented, at para. 173ff:

[Fictitious case law quotation omitted.]

The present case stands on four squares with *Norberg* and *Blank*. As set out in further detail in Tab 5, the relationship between Stone and the plaintiff was based on a power imbalance, was exploitive and arose from a breach of duty as a counsellor.

In this regard, the reports of Peter Jody Ph.D., C. Psych (Tab 6) and A.F.J. Bell, MB, BS, BHA, DPM, MRC Psych, FRANECP (Tab 7) are illuminating. The extent of the exploitation is very clear from Dr. Jody's report at page 3, where she writes:

> The abuse was intrusive and coercive in nature. It initially began by Mr. Stone instructing Ms. Jones to engage in acts such as sucking his nipples for "therapeutic" reasons. The abuse escalated to including fondling, spanking, forced exposure to pornography, fellatio, with the demand to ingest his semen. This abuse, which span for nearly two years and took place on a monthly basis, occurred in a climate of degradation and humiliation. Ms. Jones was forced to perform oral sex while in a position of powerlessness. Other degrading acts included having to kiss Mr. Stone's anus and place his testicles in her mouth. Further, Mr. Stone showed no regard for Ms. Jones, to the degree that while bedridden after her hysterectomy, Mr. Stone compelled her to perform oral sex. Beyond having to deal with the physical nature of the assaults, Ms. Jones had to cope with the reality that this abuse was being perpetrated by a person in a position of trust and authority, her therapist.

2. Liability of the Centre

The wrongful acts of Stone took place during, and as part of, grief therapy offered by the Centre. Stone was hired by the Centre to act as a counsellor although it appears he had no academic training relevant to mental health work (although it is acknowledged he obtained limited on-the-job training after being hired). Stone rose to the position of director at the Centre in spite of knowledge by an employee of the Centre that, prior to even meeting the plaintiff, but while a counsellor he "stalked" at least two of his patients. Little, if any, meaningful supervision or review of Stone's work was made by the Centre.

It is submitted the Centre is liable as principal for Stone's acts and, regardless, for failing in its duty to ensure its patients were receiving appropriate and proper treatment. Indeed, the Centre appears to have taken no steps to ensure the quality of treatment was appropriate.

3. Quantum of Damages

The report of Luke Walker C.A. (Tab 8) suggests damages for loss of income are between approximately $400,000 and $850,000. An expert for the Centre has criticized the Antman report, but has not put forth an alternative figure. The plaintiff is a qualified professional nurse who has, in effect, been deprived of her livelihood by the defendants' delicts. Dr. Jody's report suggests the cost of necessary future care is in the range of

$100,000 to $150,000 over a 20-year period. Actual expenses to date, including therapy, are in the range of $20,000.

Non-pecuniary general damages inclusive of aggravated damages are sizeable and, using the *Blank* decision as a guide, run in the range of $100,000. In this regard, the comment of the Supreme Court of Canada in *Andrews v. Grand & Toy Alberta Ltd.*, [1978] 1 W.W.R. 577 at 602 is helpful:

> There is no medium of exchange for happiness ... The monetary evaluation of non-pecuniary losses is a philosophical and policy exercise more than a legal or logical one. The award must be fair and reasonable, fairness being gauged by earlier decisions; but the award must also of necessity be arbitrary or conventional. No money can provide true restitution.

Similarly, a sizeable award of punitive damages, perhaps in the range of $25,000 (*Blank*, para. 159) is appropriate. The comments of the court in *C. v. M.* (1990), 74 D.L.R. (4th) 129 at 136 (Ont. Gen. Div.), citing *Vorvis v. I.C.B.C.* (1989), 58 D.L.R. (4th) 198 at 201-02 (S.C.C.), are helpful:

> Punitive damages, as the name would indicate, are designed to punish. In this, they constitute an exception to the general common law rule that damages are designed to compensate the injured, not to punish the wrongdoer. Aggravated damages will frequently cover conduct which could also be the subject of punitive damages but the role of aggravated damages remains compensatory.

Accordingly, judgment, exclusive of interest and costs in the range of $500,000 to $1,000,000 would seem appropriate.

Witnesses

The plaintiff anticipates calling three experts, and testifying personally. The plaintiff may call her husband to outline the current and continuing difficulties the plaintiff suffers.

The plaintiff is being examined by a medical doctor selected by the Centre. It is unclear if that doctor will testify.

Whether Stone will testify or participate fully at trial is unclear.

Length of Trial

The plaintiff anticipates trial will last five to seven days although Stone's participation at trial may affect this.

ALL OF WHICH IS RESPECTFULLY SUBMITTED

November 1, 2000
Barney C. Roubelle

ARBITRATION BRIEFS

The critical difference between an arbitration brief and a mediation brief is that an arbitrator has the power to impose a solution. Therefore, your goal is to convince the arbitrator of the merits of your case, not the party opposite. While subtlety and propriety of language is still a consideration, the purpose of an arbitration brief is to *defeat* the party opposite and not to promote settlement; winning, not accommodation, is the goal. (Are you starting to salivate at this point? Tsk tsk. That's not the spirit of ADR! Stop thinking like a lawyer!)

Arbitration briefs vary with the form of arbitration you're using. In some arbitrations, briefs are actually discouraged (or even forbidden), except as a vehicle for providing the arbitrator with documents or legal analyses. Obviously, where argument is forbidden, no argument should be submitted — to do so is considered a breach of etiquette and an insult to the arbitrator! However, when briefs are allowed, they should be prepared with care.

Here's a general "shopping list" of what an arbitration brief ought to contain:

1. A chronology of the dispute;
2. The basis of arbitration;
3. Issues in dispute and matters to be arbitrated;
4. Facts relating to the issues;
5. Evidence and the party, witness, or precedent that you want, expect or hope the trier of fact will believe;
6. Legal consideration of the issues;
7. Decisions sought (in other words, the outcome you're seeking).

Don't forget: the purpose of an arbitration brief is to persuade and prove. You're expected to refer to evidence during an arbitration, so matters that cannot be proven in the brief can be proven otherwise. Don't miss the opportunity to prove the important features of your case! Every factual submission should be backed up by a reference to a document or, at least, to anticipated evidence. Similarly, legal positions should be supported by references to case law. Set out your points the same way as you would in a factum (see Chapter 8 for further discussion on factums).

SAMPLE ARBITRATION BRIEF

Here's a typical arbitration brief:

Court File No. 99-CV-123456CM

ONTARIO
SUPERIOR COURT OF JUSTICE

B E T W E E N:

FIRED FREDDY

Plaintiff

and

SI CANADA INC., SYSTEM INCOMPETENCE TECHNOLOGIES LTD. (THAILAND), BARIUM INC., SYSTEMS INCOMPETENCE TECHNOLOGIES LIMITED (Poland), CESIUM TECHNOLOGIES INC. and SI TECHNOLOGIES, INC.

Defendants

STATEMENT OF ISSUES

(To be provided to mediator and parties at least seven days before the mediation session)

1. Factual and legal issues in dispute

1. The plaintiff is an unemployed executive who resides at Moose Factory, Ontario. The plaintiff is 51 years of age and is married. Although diligently seeking to mitigate, the plaintiff remains unemployed.

2. The defendants are corporations incorporated pursuant to various laws various jurisdictions carrying on business presently from offices in Richmond Hill, Ontario.

3. The plaintiff commenced his employment pursuant to written employment agreements on August 1, 1998, with a base annual compensation of $100,000 plus various benefits, which were of substantial value. The plaintiff was the finance manager for Canada and in that position was responsible for accounting and administrative functions and was of senior responsibility for the defendants.

4. The plaintiff, as a result of obtaining an offer of employment from the defendants, did not accept or maintain other secure employment.

5. By letter of October 28, 1999, the defendants purported to lay off the plaintiff, without payment of salary, from October 29, 1999, to a date not later than June 12, 2000.

6. The purported layoff was, in fact, merely a sham and the plaintiff pleads that the defendants intended and caused a termination of employment. The plaintiff further states that the defendants terminated the plaintiff in this fashion because they believed he would be unable to obtain recourse from the courts because of his financial difficulties

resulting from the termination. There is no legal basis to lay off an employee such as the plaintiff and the defendants have, in fact, not even pretended to call the plaintiff back to work despite his inquiry for that.

7. The defendants are presently in financial disarray and ongoing collapse with senior employees being changed almost daily. The decision makers are changing rapidly and it is unclear who is in charge. The U.S. defendant appears to be somewhat more stable and settlement direction will, presumably, come from the United States.

2. Party's Position and Interests (What the Party Hopes to Achieve)

1. Re-employment, with back pay and costs; or

2. Severance.

3. Attached documents

Attached to this form are the following documents that the plaintiff considers of central importance in the action:

1. Employment letter dated August 1, 1998;

2. Letter of Termination dated October 28, 1999.

Ima Loyyur

LOYYUR BARRISTAIR & SZAYSTAR
Barristers & Solicitors
5255 Yonge Street, Suite 810
Toronto, Ontario
M2N 6P4

Ima Loyyur (28580E)

Tel: (416) 225-2777
Fax: (416) 225-7112

Solicitors for the Plaintiff

NOTE: When the plaintiff provides a copy of this form to the mediator, a copy of the pleadings shall also be included.

NOTE: Rule 24.14 provides as follows: All communications at a mediation session and the mediator's notes and records shall be deemed to be without prejudice settlement discussions.

Freddy

- and -

SI Canada Inc., *et al.*

Court File No. 99-CV-123456CM

ONTARIO
SUPERIOR COURT OF JUSTICE
PROCEEDING COMMENCED AT TORONTO

STATEMENT OF ISSUES

LOYYUR BARRISTAIR & SZAYSTAR
Barristers & Solicitors
5255 Yonge Street, Suite 810
Toronto, Ontario
M2N 6P4

Ima Loyyur

Tel : (416) 225-2777
Fax: (416) 225-7112

Solicitors for the Plaintiff

Chapter 8

FACTUMS

NOT TO BE PICKY, BUT ...

Do good lawyers write factums?

The answer is no — good lawyers do not write factums. They write facta, which is the plural of the Latin word "factum". This said, we're going to stay grammatically incorrect in this chapter and call them "factums". After all, so do most lawyers and judges...

WHEN DO YOU NEED A FACTUM?

The word "factum" means "statement of fact and law". Generally speaking, a factum is not required for most proceedings. But even though it's not required, providing a factum is a good idea for anything more legally complex than, say, a motion to compel undertakings. The reason is the same as we've emphasized all throughout this book: When a busy master or judge gets the papers for the daily motion list, they usually pull out the notices of motion (or notices of application) to figure out which proceedings they'd like to hear. They next look to see if there are any factums filed. When they find a factum, they smile, because a factum will tell them more about the motion than any affidavit or examination transcripts can. A judicial officer — like any of us — will usually prefer to travel the path of least resistance, and that means that your motion, the one with the factum, stands a better chance than the others of being heard earlier on.

As a bonus, after the judge has read your factum, his or her preliminary view of the matter will often be influenced by it. Master Clark, Q.C., emphasized the importance of factums as follows:[1]

> Early in the morning before court begins, or even the night before, your factum will likely be read by the Court. By the time you are called upon to present your oral argument, your factum has already worked its "magic".

---

[1] B.T. Clark, Q.C. "Factums on Motions", *Preparation of Factums* (Aurora: Canada Law Book, 1996), p. 34.

The only question is whether the "magic" will have turned the lights on or turned the court off.

When you think of all the benefits of "turning the lights on", it is a foolish economy to not prepare a factum.

AUDIENCE

Like all forms of legal writing, factums have their own "audience". Actually, they have three distinct audiences. The first and most important audience is the judge considering the motion. The other two audiences are the opposing counsel and your client.

Since the primary audience for your factum is the judge, the factum's focus ought to be the judge. Any motions judge wants to know, accurately and quickly, three things: The facts of the case, what relief is being sought, and the relevant law. Accuracy and brevity are key factors. Even when a lengthy motion or application forces you to write an extensive factum, bear in mind that very lengthy factums are more likely to be skimmed through than read closely. Remember the judge's circumstances — if there is a daily list of 18 cases, the judge cannot devote more than a half hour, at most, to reviewing your case before the hearing.[2]

Make the most of your limited judicial time. Be accurate, because the best case will go off the rails if your opposition can show factual errors in your factum. Avoid the temptation to overstate your case — nothing loses a judge's favour more quickly than hyperbolic language. To touch the judge's mind and heart, you must place a premium on saying your piece accurately (warts and all), simply and clearly. It is better to sacrifice completeness if doing so avoids a lengthy factum. Remember: If your factum looks too fat, it's going to get a thin reading!

Don't make the mistake of forgetting that the remaining audiences for your factums are the opposing counsel and the client. When the other lawyer reads your factum, he or she will view your overall case from the positions you take. A clear, lucid factum that posits a strong overall case will have an intimidating effect on your opponent. If you show a lack of resolve or prepare desultory, weak materials, this will suggest a lukewarm approach or merit to your case as a whole. Good lawyers will pounce when they sense legal weakness.

The same principles apply to clients. As a successful lawyer, you must always remember that you are the proverbial "hired gun", and the clients who hire you will always be looking to see if they've gotten their money's worth. Clients want to be kept informed of what's going on, and the good ones are always watching to see if you're brilliant or a bumbler. With this in mind, can you think of a better promotional tool for your clients than a factum? A well-written factum tells the clients' story

---

[2]   I. Scott, *Appellate Advocacy in the Divisional Court* (Toronto: LSUC, 1988).

(which they know very well), lays out the applicable legal principles (which they often will not know well), and then makes a vigorous argument for the required judicial relief ("hooray for our team!"). A client will cherish a good factum — and think nothing of parting with another big retainer cheque after the hearing.

It's usually a good idea to give the client a copy of the factum and ask for his or her comments. Surprisingly, a client's comments are often a good barometer of how well your points will come across to the judge. Remember that the client has lived the case and merely needs reminding; if the client cannot understand the factum, what will a judge make of it? If your factum is incomprehensible to the client, then its content is probably not clear enough. A good test of your factum is to give it to the client and ask them to read it for 15 or 20 minutes. If the client cannot figure out clearly what you are saying in that time, then the factum needs work.

PHYSICAL LAYOUT AND FORMAT

There are certain rules concerning the form of factums, which you'll find are set out in the relevant Rules of Court. These rules cover vital details like the colour of your backsheet, the minimum sections of a factum, and any required schedules. Naturally, these procedural rules ought to be followed unless you like to live dangerously by risking the annoyance of the judge. Factums which don't comply look odd, and they instantly lose credibility for you. You do not want the court to spend time wondering where you learned your craft — let the court devote that time to learning your case!

Beyond these rules, however, there is nothing prescribing a lot of little things which can add to (or detract from) the appeal of your factum. Be choosy about your font, the use of underlining, bold and italics, tables, and how you set up case law citations. Many of today's law school graduates enter the profession knowing how to use sophisticated word processors and graphic devices, which means that there is no limit to how attractively factums can be set up. Of course, there is such a thing as overdoing it; when your embellishments cross the line from enhance-ment to distraction, it's time to tone it down. Use your good judgment, and the court may well grant you a good judgment.

The key point is that the factum must be easy to read and pleasant to look at. Many factums put their case citations in bold and transcript or case law quotations in italics. Charts (or "tables", as today's word processors call them) are very useful for organizing sequential or numerical data. Double-spacing uses more paper, but more people will read your document if you do it; double-spaced documents are easier to read. Serif fonts are easier on the eye than sans-serif, and 12-point size is nicer to read than 10-point. (Take a look at a document prepared under the new Ontario Family Law Rules to see what we mean. How eye-catching does single-spaced 10-point Arial look to you?)

STRUCTURE AND CONTENT

Sometimes the local Rules of Practice prescribe the precise form of a factum.[3] Generally, however, the form of a factum is quite loose. This lack of required structure can be put to good advantage, as it allows special situations to be given special treatment. Most times a factum needs only four elements:

1.   Introduction;
2.   Facts;
3.   Law; and
4.   Relief sought.

Some factums also require an appendix, additional "value-added" features, and all, of course, follow a standard closing. Let's take a look at each of these elements in turn.

INTRODUCTION

An introduction for a factum follows the same ground rules as writing the jumping-off lines for any other prose form: It should be simple and memorable, establishing a theme which remains in the background as the reader continues ahead. Think of the introductions you remember the best: "It was the best of times, it was the worst of times", "It was a dark and stormy night", "In Xanadu did Kubla Khan a stately pleasure dome decree."

The introduction is a chance to catch the judge's attention. It should be both clear and brief. Here are examples of the right and wrong ways to draft an introduction. They are taken from the factum for a motion for a certificate of pending litigation:

This a motion, pursuant to [relevant citation to Rules of Court], for a Certificate of Pending Litigation against lands described municipally as [location of property under dispute] and legally as:

. . .

together with a claim for costs of this motion and such further or other relief as this court may deem fit.

---

[3]   For example, appeal factums for the Court of Appeal for Ontario are required to have a summary overview paragraph.

If you haven't guessed, this is the wrong way to write an introduction. It gives the judge little relevant information (it is a certificate matter) and a lot of irrelevant information (title details, the claim for costs). Now let's try that introduction again:

This is a motion for a Certificate of Pending Litigation brought by Jim Jones ("Jones"), the plaintiff. Jones bought a house from Sam Stern ("Stern") who refused to close. Jones has sued for specific performance. Jones says the house is unique and he wants to ensure it will be available at the end of the litigation.

The second version gives the court useful information and sets the stage for the motion.

The key in the introductory paragraph is to give the judge a general idea of what the case is about without reading further. It must be accurate but not detailed — the impression of your idea is all that is needed here.

JUST THE FACTS, MA'AM

Although it seems obvious, the "Facts" section of your factum should deal only with information directly linked to the relief you're seeking. Set out the facts needed, but nothing else. For instance, on a motion to compel an attendance for discovery, it is enough to point out that the prerequisites for attendance have been met, that notice of examination was properly served, and that the witness did not attend. Facts dealing with anything else — even the substance of the case — are unnecessary and distracting.

By contrast, in a motion for summary judgment, a far fuller statement is needed and the substance of the case must be outlined. Here, brevity is less of a virtue since a motion for judgment is more significant than any other motion. The same reasoning applies as in the last example: You have to present what is legally required to earn the relief you are seeking. In a summary judgment motion, you have to throw the works into your factum, simply because you're trying to prove that you've got so much ground covered that there is no genuine issue for trial.

If you can provide some background to the case, that will be useful, provided it is limited and scrupulously fair. Here's an example of the "Facts" section for a factum in a motion in a case arising out of a failed real estate transaction. The "Facts" ought to reference facts without dwelling, at all, on the respective merits of the case. A paragraph such as the following is sufficient to place the case for the judge:

This motion arises in the context of a claim for specific performance of a real estate transaction. The plaintiff says the defendant breached the terms of the Agreement of Purchase and Sale and refused to close. The defendant says the plaintiff was never ready, willing and able to close and, in any event, failed to tender.

Provided that the facts are actually relevant, giving some detail in the factum may well be helpful. Excerpts from examination are often usefully put in a factum, provided only that the excerpts are not over-lengthy. Similarly, if specific language in a document is germane, reproduce the relevant passage in the factum. All that said, it is important not to take language out of context — misuse of quotations will certainly be caught and will greatly diminish the impact of your factum by making you look intellectually dishonest.

Similarly, where a genuine factual dispute exists, acknowledge the dispute. It is perfectly proper, indeed preferable, to have a paragraph in the "Facts" that highlights conflict rather than hides, or overlooks, the dispute. Thus, the following is preferable as giving a balanced view of the facts to a paragraph omitting an acknowledgment of a dispute:

> *The plaintiff says the share options were never granted while the defendant's evidence is that they were. As will be seen, regardless of whether or not the share options were granted, the motion for summary judgment is still proper because the issue is not material to the case as a whole.*

or

> *The husband asserts his claim for custody of the children on the grounds that the wife uses inappropriate discipline. He cites as a particular example an incident in February 2000, when the five-year-old daughter was hospitalized with a concussion. The husband claims that this injury resulted from the wife slapping the child's forehead, while the wife attributes the injury to the child playing parachute in the basement.*

Remember: State the facts fairly and use neutral language — to do otherwise insults the Bench and injures your case.

Unless the "Facts" section is very short, it likely makes sense to group the factual assertions into subgroups with headings. These subgroups can be defined chronologically (*e.g.*, "Before Breach", "After Arrest", "Custody Arrangements Prior to Interim Separation Agreement") or by legal relevance (*e.g.*, "*Ex Juris* Issues", "Reasonable and Probably Grounds for Arrest", "Children's Interests"). The way the subgrouping is established is less important than establishing the facts — the goal is the reader's understanding of the necessary facts as quickly and simply as possible. Try to keep the "Facts" section short — if possible limit it to a minimum of four pages. Cases do exist that need more detailed facts, but such cases, even at the appellate level, are few.

LAW

Very few cases raise more than one or two novel issues of law. Most of the time, the legal principles are scarcely in dispute and the only issue for the judge is to apply the facts to uncontested law. Accordingly, the "Law" section should really be limited to a brief and clear statement of the relevant law, be it case law, statute or textual, and a statement of how the law applies to the facts. Similar to the circumstance in which you had to deal with harmful facts, where there is law against your position, cite the law and then try to distinguish it. Failing to disclose bad law makes your research look sloppy at best, and greatly diminishes the power of your factum.

Many counsel believe in taking a minimalistic approach to the "Law" section of their factums. They advocate omitting all legal principles that are not truly contentious. According to this theory, trite law is unhelpful and distracting. Thus, Master Clark, a leading counsel, says:[4]

> *counsel should select carefully what they cite so as to focus the court's attention exclusively on the points that are in actual dispute. For instance, do not cite law that is trite: it will trivialize your submission.*

There was a brief experiment in the 1990s when one Ontario court insisted on litigants submitting factums for every motion. The practice soon ceased because there was so much trite law in the factums that the judges refused to read them!

Certainly, it is sensible to carefully select what you wish to draw to the court's attention. For example, in a case dealing with the "postal acceptance" rule, the court does not need a general review of the law on offer and acceptance in contract. Nevertheless, a court should be made aware of the general legal context of the proceeding before it, as well as being reminded of its jurisdiction to make the order sought. Even if it is self-evident that the court can make the order sought, outline where that authority comes from. Here's an example:

> *The appeal before the court relates to the actions of the arresting officer, who coerced a confession from the appellant by threats of torture. The appellant asks the court to declare the confession inadmissible as evidence, pursuant to section 24(2) of the Canadian Charter of Rights and Freedoms, in that it was obtained in a manner that infringed the appellant's rights, and having regard to all the circumstances, the admission of it would bring the administration of justice into disrepute.*

Reference to case law should be limited. Very few factums need more than two or three cases, and to make sure that these are read by the judge, highlight the key passages with a suitably bright colour. This will not insult the judge; he or she will probably be grateful for your assistance. If, by contrast, you cite 15 to 20 cases, you can assume they will not be read.

Another issue that counsel differ on is the presence of written legal argument. Generally speaking, factums are not supposed to include argument; if you do this clumsily, you will not impress the court. That said, somewhat more subtle argument can and should be included in a factum. It's all a question of packaging. The general order of this kind of argument is:

---

4 B.T. Clark, Q.C., "Factums on Motions", *Preparation of Factums* (Aurora: Canada Law Book, 1996), p. 40.

1. Statement of law;
2. Reference to facts of case; and
3. Conclusion.

The phrasing you use is something along the lines of:

1. Under modern Canadian law ...
2. In the instant case, the plaintiff ..., and
3. Accordingly, it is respectfully submitted that ...

The argument is subtle enough not to be distracting, but relates the law and facts together to come to a conclusion. Here's an example:

1. Definition of a Weapon

"weapon" means anything used, designed to be used, or intended for use

    (a) in causing death or injury to any person, or

    (b) for the purpose of threatening or intimidating any person

and, without restricting the generality of the foregoing, includes a firearm as defined in subsection 84(1);

Criminal Code of Canada, s. 2.

2. For the purposes of this Part,

"firearm" means a barrelled weapon from which any shot, bullet or other projectile can be discharged and that is capable of causing serious bodily injury or death to a person, and includes any frame or receiver of such a barrelled weapon and anything that can be adapted for use as a firearm;

Criminal Code of Canada, s. 84(1).

3. The issue of intent is relevant to the interpretation of "weapon" as it is defined in s. 2 of the Criminal Code; "...[An] innocuous article, if used or intended for use in causing death or injury to persons, could constitute a weapon. It is not the design of the object but the state of mind of the possessor which converts it into a weapon".

Clark J. in R. v. Kilpatrick (1986), 31 C.C.C. (3d) 334 (Ont. Dist. Ct.).

4. It is the respectful submission of the Appellant that no evidence was adduced at trial which showed beyond a reasonable doubt that his possession of the plastic replica handgun and the X-acto knife was "intended for use for the purpose of threatening or intimidating any person".

5. It is the further respectful submission of the appellant that the evidence adduced at trial did not prove beyond a reasonable doubt that the plastic replica handgun fitted the definition of being a "barrelled weapon from which any shot, bullet, or other projectile can be discharged and that is capable of causing serious bodily injury or death to a person".

RELIEF SOUGHT

The final section of a factum is a statement of what you want the court to do. Sometimes merely repeating the relief sought from the notice of motion or notice of appeal will do, but this often changes. A careful statement of what is now wanted is important and, if more limited than earlier materials suggested, shows how reasonable your position is. Indeed, even a respondent can do well here by agreeing to inevitable relief, and asking only that questionable relief be denied. Here's an example:

Accordingly, the applicant asks that honourable court for:

1. *an Order finding the husband in contempt, and committing him to jail if he does not take steps to purge his contempt;*

2. *a further Order requiring the husband to pay forthwith the costs assessed against him in the Order of Her Honour Madame Justice Boyko;*

3. *a further Order requiring the husband to pay forthwith all arrears of child support;*

4. *costs to the wife on a solicitor/client basis, to be paid forthwith;*

5. *such further and other order as seems just to this honourable court.*

APPENDIX

Sometimes you have materials that are lengthy, and which would detract from the flow of your factum, but nevertheless ought to be included in the factum in some fashion. The materials may be a detailed chronology of events, a paragraph-by-paragraph refuting of the allegations made by the party opposite, or perhaps a chart showing how prior cases have dealt with damages in similar cases.

Regardless of the nature of the material, putting it in the factum proper will ensure that the factum itself is not read, or is read reluctantly. The appropriate way to deal with such material is to reference it briefly in the factum and then attach the material as an appendix. Appendices can be ignored or just glanced at if the judge doesn't have the time or desire to wade through them. If the court is interested, it will review the material and, if not, the attachment of an appendix will not hurt the factum.

"ADDED VALUE" FEATURES

Remember: The primary focus of a factum is to make a judge rule in your favour — if you can make this easier for the court, you will win more cases. To help the court see things in your favour, some "added value" features can be incorporated in factums. These special features include:

1. Case law excerpts, especially on computer disk;
2. Transcript excerpts, especially on computer disk;
3. Text of the factum on computer disk;
4. Legal memoranda, especially on computer disk; and
5. Important exhibits (say, contracts) in a brief on a computer disk.

Notice something about that list? Common to all these features is "on computer disk". Why not? Transcripts are usually prepared on computers, and most cases can easily be downloaded easily from computer research facilities, or scanned from "hard copy". From there, it's a simple task to copy them to a floppy and submit it along with your factum. Obviously, the factum itself and legal memorandum prepared in your office can be downloaded to disk. (Some caution should be used with legal memoranda to ensure that nothing privileged or not before the court is accidentally disclosed.)

Modern judges are, as a rule, computer literate and secretary-deprived. The days when every judge had a secretary are long gone, and it is increasingly common for judges to prepare and type their own judgments. So "go with the flow" and attach a floppy disk. The judge will appreciate having blocks of text in a user-friendly form that can be "plugged in" to judgments without copy typing. Since the blocks of text available on your computer disk are, on balance, favourable to your case, having the judge adopt such text as their own can only be to your benefit.

Obviously, if your text is going to be helpful to the judge, it must be in a form the court can use. Remember that most judges do not have leading-edge technology. The most basic computer language reasonably available should be used — ASCII text is probably best, as it is likely readable by whatever system the court uses.

THE RIGHT WAY TO END

Always end your factum like this:

ALL OF WHICH IS RESPECTFULLY SUBMITTED.

IMA LOYYUR

Solicitor for the [Plaintiff or Defendant]

And, with our respectful submission, that's all for this chapter.

Chapter 9

WRITTEN ARGUMENT AT TRIAL

INTRODUCTION

Written argument during trial is fairly unusual in Canadian civil practice. In cases with claims that are lengthy or particularly technical, written argument may be asked for by the court,[1] but most counsel do not deliver written argument at a trial without judicial urging. This approach is a mistake. Delivering good written materials at trial gives counsel an extra chance at winning the case. Counsel who submit a written argument are, in effect, keeping their legal arguments going long after they've finished making verbal submissions. This advantage pays off even after the trial is over, whether or not the judge reserves the ruling. And even if there is no reserve, written argument directs the court's thinking in productive ways.

The main arguments lawyers make against preparing written argument are about time and uncertainty. During a trial, they say, there is no time to prepare elaborate written materials. And why prepare anything in advance when it will probably be useless for closing, because trials almost never turn out as expected? Neither argument stands up to analysis, of course — the lawyer just doesn't feel like doing the work.

Time is not really a factor because you'll already be drafting closing arguments during trial, and your written submissions will be almost identical. The time it takes to double-up matching written materials (which need not be extensive) is modest. As far as uncertainty goes, yes, it's true that trials tend to develop in unforeseen ways, but they're not usually that far from what you expected. Have you ever seen a claim for corporate oppression suddenly morph into a personal injury case? Not likely. You may not know if a specific claim or defence will be proven, but you will certainly know what evidence there is in support of the other side's position, and you can easily figure out the legal argument that they will try to squeeze out of it.

---

[1] For example, *Schwartz v. Stone*, 1998 Carswell Ont. 3480, online: *e*Carswell <http://www.ecarswell.com>.

BEFORE CLOSING

Some judges refuse written argument before all the evidence is heard, on the basis that such argument might improperly bias their analysis of the evidence. Other judges will accept written submissions at the start of trial. Regardless, all judges will accept a brief of authorities at the start of trial. A brief of authorities is a compendium of case law and excerpts from widely accepted legal books; for example, if you have a case where a key witness will be testifying about something she heard a child say, your brief of authorities might have the text of *R. v. Khan*, [1990] 2 S.C.R. 531, and also the appropriate section from Sopinka, Lederman and Bryant's *The Law of Evidence is Canada*, 2d ed. There might well be shorter references to these materials in the factum you filed earlier on, and they might have whetted the court's appetite to read more. Give the judges what they crave!

A word of caution: Many counsel go overboard and deliver immense briefs, in multiple volumes, containing dozens of cases. A judge is almost as busy at trial as counsel is — so the court's likely reaction will be to read only a little bit and use the casebook as a paperweight. Limit yourself to perhaps four or five cases, articles or textbook passages if you want a judge to look at it. Be sure to include an index, complete with headings that explain the purpose of each passage. Here's a sample casebook index, taken from a case whose issues are oppression and fundamental breach:

Court File No. 27589/01

COURT OF QUEEN'S BENCH

B E T W E E N:

LOU'S LIVELY LIQUORS

Plaintiff

- and -

MULEKICK DISTILLERIES

Defendant

BOOK OF AUTHORITIES

Document*	TAB
Case Law on Fundamental Breach	
Goldblatt v. Closed Window Bakeries [1982] 32 O.R. (7th) 423	1

---

*   All case law cited here is fictitious.

BOOK OF AUTHORITIES (cont.)

Zithers Department Stores v. Thompson
  [1996] 24 A.L.R. (8th) 826   2

G. Kay v. Scalpers Hair Salons
  [2000] 2 D.L.R. (5th) 10   3

Case Law on Oppression

2873645 Canada Inc. v. Sharma
  [1979] 18 N.S.R. (6th) 3   4

Moses v. Pharoahcorp
  [1450 B.C.] 1 All Egy. R. 22   5

Document   TAB

Legal Authorities

Syd Silver on Breaches (excerpt)   6

Oppression For Fun and Profit (excerpt)   7

As you can see from the above, a brief of authorities, containing, say, two items dealing with oppression and two or three with fundamental breach is appropriate. Pick textbook extracts and a recent leading case. Be sure to also use careful highlighting of relevant passages to lead the court's attention in useful directions without committing to what the evidence will be.

On the whole, we recommend against submitting written argument before all the evidence is in. Surprises do happen at trial, and not all claims or defences will be established at the close of testimony. If you've already submitted written materials respecting those claims or defences that you could not prove, the judge will be reading something that is irrelevant and, what is worse, may give credibility to otherwise meritless positions by your opponent.

AFTER THE EVIDENCE

Here's a useful trial hint: If at all possible, try to get an overnight recess between the last witness and closing argument. Obviously, by the time all the evidence is in, you have, or ought to have, a good idea about what to argue in closing. By preparing a written argument you can have the judge both hear and read your closing argument. And don't forget, in the event that the decision is reserved, the written argument also serves as a continuing advocate in the judge's chambers.

Like a factum, your written argument will include a combination of facts and law. The facts you allude to will come from the evidence adduced at the just-completed trial. When drafting the "Facts" portion of your written argument, remember that the judge has heard the same evidence as you have. Asserting facts that were not proven is not going to do anything more than insult the court; you can only work with what you have, so be very straightforward. A short but fair factual review — perhaps highlighting points that were somewhat subtle — is as far as you want to go. If your summary is drafted simply and fairly, the court may be inclined to accept your version of the facts in the reasons for judgment.

In the legal section of your argument, you can be more expansive. Elaborate on the law and, if necessary, add case law and authorities to those previously submitted. Focus as closely as possible on the facts of the case at trial. Broadly stated propositions of law are not as helpful as pinpointing cases that are similar to the one before the judge. Try to limit your case law and authorities. Don't try to beat the judge over the head with case after case on the same legal point. Remember: The judge usually doesn't mind your help in writing reasons for his or her judgment, so give the judge suitable material to do it in your favour.

As we advised in the last chapter, it's often very helpful to include a floppy disk of your argument with your materials. If your argument is reasonably fair, the court may consider using it as the basis of its own reasons; in such a case the court may take your argument on disk and excerpt it into the reasons.

Sample Written Argument (Close of Trial)

By way of illustration, an example of written argument delivered at the close of trial follows:

WRITTEN ARGUMENT OF THE DEFENDANTS

Introduction

- From spring 1997 until summer 1998 the plaintiff was a distributor of environmentally friendly cleaning and disinfecting productions of the defendant PEN. This distribution was made pursuant to a written agreement dated April 21, 1997.
- The plaintiff says that PEN did not honour the distributorship agreement and committed a fundamental breach. The plaintiff also claims that the defendants have acted oppressively.
- The plaintiff also says that, shortly after the distribution agreement was signed, the quality of products fell markedly, at least in terms of packaging.

Facts and Evidence

- Five witnesses testified. The plaintiff called Richard Howe, principal of the plaintiff; Jim Shalom, who sells PEN products; and Don McDonald, who sold PEN products. The defendants called Paul Murphy, a principal of PEN; and Edward Rogers, who works for PEN.

- The following facts are uncontested:
  1. The products worked adequately or well; indeed, the plaintiff repeatedly expressed the view that some of the products were of high quality.
  2. Other persons were able to sell the products profitably.
  3. The plaintiff sold the products for over a year, albeit with disappointing results, and exercised his credits and other rights under the distributorship agreement.
  4. The distribution agreement was prepared by counsel for the plaintiff, albeit with input from PEN.
  5. Mr. Howe has 25 years of working experience and eight years of experience in business. He has post-secondary education. Mr. Howe signed the distributorship agreement in trust because he wished to avoid personal liability. Mr. Murphy has extensive business experience but only grade-school education.

- No evidence of an expert was tendered by the plaintiff.
- The plaintiff did produce numerous bottles of product, but did not say when each particular bottle was produced or received. Although PEN product was often sold in large, commercial-sized containers no large container, or photograph of large container, was produced. In cross-examination, the plaintiff acknowledged that the bottles that were produced, or some of them, were selected from an unspecified larger group to show specific defects. The bottles, or at least some of them, were previously opened and only partially full. Evidence as to how they were stored or what had happened to the part of the product used was rough at best.
- Jim Shalom said that the products performed perfectly well and that he made money selling them. He saw no decrease in quality or irregularity in production during a relevant time; indeed, he suggested the products had improved somewhat. Don McDonald gave up the sale of PEN products because they were not selling well; this problem he suggested was that society was not ready for environmentally friendly products such as PEN sells. Edward Rogers said the quality of the products has not changed since he became involved with PEN. None of these witnesses is a party, although it is acknowledged that Mr. Rogers works for PEN.

Complaints

- The plaintiff's complaints at trial relate to (a) labelling problems (b) colouring problems (c) technical support problems and (d) issues about the plastic bottles product came in.
- With regard to the labelling problems the defendants note that:

    1. for reasons that were unclear, the plaintiff bought blank labels. No explanation of why the plaintiff would need blank labels was offered and the uncontradicted testimony of PEN was that no bottle left PEN unlabelled. While the plaintiff said some labels were inferior it did not suggest bottles were ever unlabelled. While the evidence is equivocal and in conflict, there is some suggestion that some bottles produced in evidence do not bear labels of PEN or Storage Canada, PEN's predecessor; and

    2. the most significant labelling problems related to product bearing a label naming Storage Canada. These bottles bore a simple computer-generated label. Storage Canada stopped being part of the distribution of products very shortly after the distribution agreement was executed; the court is reminded that the plaintiff testified he had no problems with product in that period.

- In terms of colouring problems, the evidence was that sometimes products that were normally blue were blue-green. No claim that this affected the products' utility was made.
- Technical support was complained of by the plaintiff. That said, the plaintiff spoke of four or five manuals or binders of materials that he received, but failed to produce at trial. He also described numerous discussions with PEN seeking sales and other advice.
- Finally, the plastic bottle problem (slightly collapsed bottles) was not raised in the pleadings, discovery or initial complaint letter. In cross-examination, the plaintiff acknowledged the deformation of the bottles might have happened while they were being stored and not when picked up from PEN.

Elements of Cause of Action and Breach of Contract

- It is axiomatic that the plaintiff must establish the cause of action asserted. Here the basic claim is for a fundamental breach of contract.
- The distributorship agreement contains two terms allegedly breached. These are

    6. *Obligations of SCI:*

During the currency of this Agreement, the SCI covenants and agrees that it shall:

...

(b) *provide the services listed in Schedule "C" attached hereto and give to the Distributor such assistance in advertising, instructions in servicing and such aid generally as the Company gives to its other Distributors;*

(c) *use its best efforts to deliver uniform quality of the Products ...*

- The technical support as described in the distributorship agreement's Schedule "C". No evidence was led suggesting that the items in that schedule were not provided.

- The only concern respecting uniformity raised was that of colour of product. It is respectfully submitted that the slight variation of blue to blue-green is minor at best and the products fall inside the ambit of "best efforts to deliver uniform product" as set out in the distributorship agreement. The general quality of the products was not challenged by any witness.

- More generally, the exclusive territory given by the distributorship agreement was granted to the plaintiff and the plaintiff was able to exercise, and did exercise, his financial credits under the agreement. The plaintiff made sales and, if the sales were slow, the evidence of Mr. Shalom suggests this lack of sales was the result of the plaintiff not properly or fully following up with sales leads. Regardless, the sales of product were the responsibility of the plaintiff and not PEN.

- Finally, while the burden of proof is to only a civil standard, much of the plaintiff's evidence was vague as to numbers and details, and consisted of generalities. Indeed, the plaintiff did not even clarify what products he bought, or when, or in what quantity. The value of product retained by the plaintiff, which the plaintiff acknowledges must be accounted for, is unclear at best. A plaintiff must put forth an orderly case proving its damages clearly. That has not been done here.

Fundamental Breach

- The decision in Kordas v. Stokes, 1992 Carswell 156 (Ont. C.A.), online: *e*carswell <http://www.ecarswellcom> sets out the test for a fundamental breach. There must be a complete failure to deliver that which was promised and such failure must arise in the context of unconscionability (see para. 24).

- Here it cannot be said that the plaintiff received something fundamentally different from what he bargained for. The plaintiff received a territorial right to market what are, by all accounts, good products. The defects, if any, in the products related to labels (and then mostly to product produced by the predecessor to PEN) and minor variation in colour from batch to batch. Such defects, even if proven, hardly amount to a total failure of consideration.

- In terms of inequality of bargaining power, the court is reminded that the plaintiff was represented by counsel, unlike PEN, and, in terms of business and education, PEN does not have any advantage over the plaintiff. Indeed, in terms of experience and professional guidance, the evidence before the court suggests the plaintiff was more sophisticated than PEN. This is not a case of a strong party overreaching.

Mitigation

- Although the plaintiff referred to efforts to sell the products it still has, no particulars of mitigation have been adduced.
- More importantly, no effort of any sort to sell the rights under the distributorship agreement was demonstrated. Paragraph 29 of the agreement allows for the assignment of the agreement, albeit with consent such consent not to be unreasonably withheld.

Oppression

- The oppression remedy is very broad and would allow the imposition of liability in cases where the corporate veil might shield directors (*Budd v. Gentra*, 1998 Carswell 3069 (Ont. C.A.), para. 47), online: *e*carswell<http://www.ecarswellcom>. That said, the Court of Appeal has expressed concern the remedy may be sought on occasion as a tactic only (*Budd, supra,* para. 50). Certainly, some act involving an improper abuse of corporate governance is needed for oppression to apply (*Budd, supra,* paras. 32, 33).
- It is acknowledged that the Court has an almost unlimited discretionary power under the oppression remedy but it is submitted that, in this case, even if a breach of contract is found, no element of the misuse of corporate power *qua* corporate power exists and, accordingly, the oppression remedy is inappropriate.

USING THE WRITTEN ARGUMENT

In virtually all cases, the trial judge does not receive the written argument until the day of closing. This means that, if the written argument is to have maximum effect, you must give it to the judge at the start of your summation, and then refer to it during argument. Do not read the argument — the court can do that well enough — but follow the written argument's structure and, as you make oral argument, let the court know where you are in your written argument.

Make your submissions slowly enough for the court to be able to read the relevant passage from the written argument without missing anything important. Saying something like, "Your Honour, my next concern is [describe your point] and I deal with this at paragraphs 31 and 32 of the written argument", is quite effective, especially if you give the court time to read the two paragraphs. The court will now have your submissions in both sight and sound.

"CLOSING ARGUMENT" ON WRITTEN ARGUMENTS

Written argument during trial is an effective way to reinforce your case. Some people wrongly call it a form of cheating. It is not. Written argument is yet another example of diligent and careful work that will pay off for those advocates who know how to maximize their chances of success at trial.

Chapter 10

APPEALS

INTRODUCTION

Yes, you are an outstanding barrister. Yes, your advocacy is always first-rate. Yes, your presence alone is enough to make your clients the odds-on favourite to win the hearing, no matter how bad their position. But in spite of all these overwhelming advantages, the unthinkable happens every now and then: You lose the hearing and have to go before an appellate court to obtain the justice your client so richly deserves. Appellate writing is the focus of this chapter.

Appeals differ from hearings of first instance in important ways: (1) the evidentiary record is fixed,[1] and (2) there is a presumption that the decision being considered is correct. These two factors considerably cut down your scope for written advocacy. You can no longer prepare any new affidavits, which emphasizes the importance of what you already have to work with.

Appellate judges have a very real grasp on the costs (both financial and emotional) of litigation. They are predisposed to seek financial and emotional finality for the parties to the litigation. Therefore, in order for an appeal to have any chance of success, the appellant must grab the court's attention right away. Grab the judge's attention before the hearing — in the factums and appeal books.

Although practice varies from court to court, most appellate judges get the appeal materials a week or so before the hearing. Often, the appeal materials are given to a law clerk to summarize, leaving the judges with only a distillation of fact and argument. Even with this assistance, the appellate judge has little time to review the appeal in detail. Many appeals panels have a "triage" system similar to hospital emergency wards. After a quick scan at what an upcoming appeal is all about, the judges categorise it right away as: (1) definitely of interest; (2) moderately interesting; or (3) hopeless and a waste of time. If an appeal is put into the "hopeless" pile, virtually no chance of success remains. Since most appeals really are without merit, counsel must ensure that the

---

[1] Subject to the rare situation where fresh evidence is adduced.

merits of the appeal at hand (regardless of its real strength) stand out strongly.

The first item the court looks at is always the notice of appeal. Too many counsel assume the notice of appeal is *pro forma* and draft something quick and filled with boilerplate. A boilerplate notice of appeal is definitely unhelpful. In fact, it's counter-productive, since boilerplate puts the judges to sleep when your overriding objective is to wake them up. So prepare a proper and persuasive notice or, if that is not possible, amend and file a full notice before the materials go to the appellant judges. Remember: You don't get a second chance to make a good first impression.

Once the notice of appeal is reviewed, the appellate court reads the judgment or charge of the court below. Since this is a given, little advocacy comes into play here. Most judges then read the law clerk's summary. These items give the judge an idea about the case and, usually, a preliminary view as to how to rule.

Finally, the judge opens the factums. It is worth emphasizing that most judges do not read the appeal factums until they have read quite a bit of other material. The judge does not come to the factums without at least a preliminary knowledge of the case. Anything in the factum that is glaringly wrong will immediately leap out, so be especially careful when drafting factums for high courts. Put another way, the factum must be consistent with the notice of appeal and the judgment or charge.

NOTICE OF APPEAL

The format of a notice of appeal is deceptively straightforward. Regardless of the relevant Rules of Practice, all notices of appeal provide the following information: (1) the court appealed from and appealed to; (2) what the appellant wants the appellate court to do; and (3) the grounds for the appeal. Notices of appeal, or related certificates, also set out what evidence is to be relied on during the appeal. While each element of a notice of appeal seems rather obvious, you should know by now that there's more to it than that. With a little subtlety, you can get the notice of appeal to work for you.

A point to keep in mind is that a notice of appeal ought to be a self-contained document that can be read and understood without other material. A detailed, but cryptic, notice will annoy, not persuade, an appellate judge.

CHOOSING THE RIGHT COURT

In theory, you rarely get to choose the court you appeal to. In criminal cases, the *Criminal Code* guides you up a very short appellate path, with a short-cut if the Crown proceeded by indictment. In civil proceedings, the correct appellate court is clear as soon as you commit to a particular amount in dispute. But there is one situation where the matter is not always clear: Those times when you're unsure about the nature of the order being appealed. Is it final, or is it interlocutory?

Difficulty in determining what is final as opposed to interlocutory crops up more often than you might think. The nature of some orders is a no-brainer — if the court orders the statement of claim struck, that's about as final as you can get. An order regarding discovery? That's almost certainly interlocutory. The judgment after trial is *really* final. That said, what about an order adding a party? Final or interlocutory? An order refusing an amendment? The test of whether an issue raised in the litigation is finally disposed of is hard to apply, and most orders can be viewed as final or interlocutory — depending on how the issue is phrased.

If the difference between an interlocutory or final order does not affect where and how an appeal from that order is heard, then the question is rather academic. But sometimes there's a big difference. Many times, an appeal from a final order is heard without leave of the court. An appeal from an interlocutory order, however, can be heard by the court only with leave. More significantly, appeals from final orders go to one court, while appeals from interlocutory orders go to a different court.

When you're faced with bringing your appeal to one court or another, you can often make an intelligent guess about which court is more likely to grant your appeal, and which court will resent even having to hear it. If bringing your appeal to one court or another is likely to be dispositive (*e.g.*, if you are comfortable that one court will dismiss your appeal while another court might allow it), consider whether you can shoehorn your appeal into a form that the court you prefer can accept. This means you'll have to add some paragraphs in your grounds for appeal, justifying your presence there and explaining why you have chosen one court over another. Phrasing like the following is helpful:

> *The decision below finally disposed of the issue of* [list issue] *and so this appeal is from a final order. Accordingly, this appeal is brought to the* [relevant appellate court], *pursuant to* [relevant rule].

The presence of this phrase in your notice of appeal ensures that the court knows why you are bringing the appeal where you are. Even if the court disagrees with you on its jurisdiction, this phrase will still convey the impression that you're a thoughtful counsel worth listening to.

RELIEF SOUGHT

All too often, notices of appeal treat the "Relief Sought" section as mere boilerplate. This is a mistake. Think about it: This is the section where you are actually telling the court what it needs to do for you. Judges are human, too; how do you feel when a stranger comes to you asking for the moon? Except in cases where it is clearly justified (and these are rare), appellate courts seldom reverse a lower court's decision completely. Asking for something unlikely to be given is unpersuasive and weakens the entire notice of appeal. Without being overly detailed, think about what you need from the appeal, what you can legitimately argue the first instance judge did wrong, and then base your relief sought on that.

Here are two "Relief Sought" examples. You decide which one is more likely to be taken seriously:

RELIEF SOUGHT:

1. *An order setting aside the conviction.*

2. *A further order for a new trial.*

3. *Such further and other order as seems just to this Honourable Court.*

or

RELIEF SOUGHT:

1. *An order setting aside the conviction.*

2. *A further order substituting an acquittal for the conviction.*

3. *A further order finding bias on the part of the jury.*

4. *A further order requiring the Crown to pay for the appellant's victory party at a good hotel.*

5. *A further order requiring that the learned trial judge be tarred-and-feathered.*

6. *Such further and other order as seems just to the appellant.*

Obviously, the second "Relief Sought" is better.

As previously mentioned, a notice of appeal ought to be a self-contained document that can be read and understood without reading the other material relating to the case at hand. Accordingly, the grounds for relief should briefly set out enough of the case to allow the judge reading the notice of appeal to understand what the appeal is all about. At a minimum, the grounds ought to include:

1. A description of the parties and the case;
2. What the first instance judge did;
3. What was wrong with what happened in the court below; and
4. Relevant statutory or regulatory provisions that support your appeal.

Be specific in what you say. "The learned trial judge erred in finding no genuine issue for trial" says very little; on the other hand, "the judge weighed evidence of parties in the absence of *viva voce* evidence" tells the appeal court what actually happened. Try to ensure that your notice is not too detailed. A good test is to give the notice to someone who is unfamiliar with the case, ask him or her to read the notice for no more than a couple of minutes and tell you what the appeal is all about. Remember: If a literate person cannot understand the basis of the appeal in two minutes or less, the notice is too complex.

Most grounds for appeal conclude with a basket provision reading something like this: "Such further or other grounds as counsel may advise and this Honourable Court accepts." This sentence is usually a waste of time, since you're clever enough to know your grounds for appeal by the time you're drafting the notice. Nevertheless, put it in, just so you can ward off a later argument of "Counsel is covering new grounds not set out in the notice of appeal!"

Finally, consider how long your notice of appeal actually is. There is a tendency for some counsel to draft lengthy notices of appeal that are very detailed. As we all know by now, however, such notices tend to be skimmed over by the court. Good points get lost if they're buried in an overly long notice of appeal, so remember its purpose — to let the judge know what the appeal is about. The *factum* is the document that you should cram full of detail.

APPEAL BOOKS AND APPEAL MATERIALS

Each appellate court has a special set of procedural rules governing the format of appeal books. Some courts have formats that mirror the first hearing court whereas others, such as the Supreme Court of Canada, have strikingly unusual binding and formatting requirements. These points may seem petty (and, let's face it, they are), but if an appeal is to be given any chance of success, its materials must conform with standard practice. Take the time to review the requirements of an unfamiliar court or, if finances allow, hire a lawyer who is familiar with the practice to put together the materials. Judges sitting on appeal courts were usually extremely competent counsel when they were lawyers in practice. You can bet they submitted impeccable materials to the courts where they are now sitting as judges, so it's quite possible that they will take irregular documents as an insult. Even if the court doesn't raise the issue of irregular documentation directly, it will be noticed and held against their impressions of counsel and the merits of the appeal.

FACTUMS ON APPEAL

Appellate court judges do not come to the factum on appeal without some background. Most judges have enough experience to have a preliminary opinion on the legal issue you're bringing before them. Accordingly, the appeal factum has to start with enough vigour to inspire the judge to read it carefully; not simply to skim over the material to reinforce his or her existing impressions. Even if the judge is predisposed to your view of the law, it is still important to chauffeur him or her to the conclusion you want. This means drafting a clear and easily digested statement of what the case is about and what should be done, and placing it right up front.

Appeal factums differ.from motion or application factums in that their focus is more legal, and the appellate court has more time and patience for legal argument. While brevity is a prerequisite in motion or application factums, completeness is more important in an appeal factum. This will be your last chance to influence the court — do not omit material that may help. However, unless your material is compelling, it may lose the court's attention. A complete factum reviews the facts and law thoroughly, but does so without repetition or unnecessary text. You can assume that the appellate court has read the reasons for judgment or charge to jury from the lower-level court closely, and so, while the factum ought to stand alone, it is unnecessary to rehash details that have no impact on the appeal. Focus on all the necessary facts, but nothing more.

The same organizational rules of other legal writing apply to appeal factums. Grouping the facts together into subgroups with headings is helpful and makes reading easier. These subgroups can be defined chronologically (*e.g.*, "Before Breach", "After Arrest", "Custody Arrangements Prior to Interim Separation Agreement"), or by legal relevance (*e.g.*, "Ex Juris Issues", "Reasonable and Probably Grounds for Arrest", "Children's Interests"). How you organize your subgroups is less important than that you establish them clearly — the goal is to allow the reader to understand the necessary facts as simply as possible.

Legal analysis in appeal factums is generally more extensive than at first instance. Unlike most lower courts, appeal courts tend to be receptive to academic pieces suggesting changes in the law. (After all, higher courts are where precedent-setting and binding interpretations take place.) While your legal analysis ought to be grounded in case law — and such case law need not be restricted to your province or even to Canada — you can also include academic proposals for legal development if they help your case.

Finally, an appeal factum, regardless of what the relevant Rules of Practice say, must include an argument. Statements of law are the building blocks, but they're meaningless unless they help you erect the edifice of your appellate case. By themselves, they are unpersuasive. The better approach is to begin with a general statement of law as it exists, followed, where appropriate, by a summary of academic opinion on how the law ought to develop, and then relating these statements to the facts before the court. Here's an example:

> *Rule 25.11 states that a court may strike out all or part of a pleading on the grounds that the pleading is scandalous, frivolous or vexatious, or an abuse of the process of the court. In recent jurisprudence, the definition of these key words has been expanded to include situations where the facts pleaded are obviously false and slanderous. This is an appeal of the lower court's ruling which allowed the defendant to retain certain statements in his statement of defence, even though he had previously sworn under oath the exact opposite of what he pleaded. The effect of these statements remaining in the statement of defence is to completely change the characterisation of the appellant plaintiff's interactions with the defendant from that of innocent victim to co-aggressor.*

USE OF MATERIALS AT HEARING

Sometimes it is clear that the court of appeal has not reviewed the appeal materials or factums in detail (no doubt due to pressure of heavy caseloads). It won't take long for you to realize that the court has only the haziest idea of what the case is about. Many counsel throw up their hands at times like these, and come to the view that their efforts on written advocacy have been a total waste of time. Far from it! In cases where the court has not read the materials closely, carefully written clear materials become a tremendous tool.

Remember, as a touchstone, that you should always take care to avoid annoying the court. If the court has reviewed your written materials in depth, dwelling on them will be tedious for the court and may do nothing more than allow the court time to think of reasons why your written materials are weak. But where the court has not read the materials fully, go slowly and walk the court through the materials. Do not reread your materials — the judges can do that — but stop at each paragraph and make slow oral submissions on each one, beginning with a phrase like, "turning then to paragraphs 19 through 22 of our factum, to the question of…". Say inconsequential things to allow the court to read your factum's passages without missing anything important, and then make your substantive submissions. In this way the court has your submissions in sight and sound; this combination can be very effective.

Sometimes an ill-prepared court can be of great benefit!

TECHNOLOGY

Appellate courts usually have more support staff per judge than courts of first instance. Nevertheless, appeal judges, when possible, try to economize on secretarial use and many judges prepare a rough draft of reserve decisions on their own computer. With increasing computer literacy, more judges will prepare their own documents. Accordingly, any saving of computer effort will be appreciated. It is prudent (where permitted) to file a computer disk containing the text of your factum and, if you act for the appellant, the notice of appeal. Assuming your arguments find favour with the court, large parts of your factum may find their way into the final decision. Even if your legal arguments are not accepted, a fair and even-handed (and drafted from your client's perspective) adoption of your facts can be helpful in softening a loss or on a subsequent appeal.

Chapter 11

Written Advocacy before Administrative Tribunals

HOW TRIBUNALS DIFFER FROM COURTS

On the surface, tribunals and courts seem to be very similar: They both hear adversarial proceedings, they make legally binding determinations, and you have to prepare submissions on fact and law. Certainly, there are strong similarities between courts and tribunals, but there are also important differences, and these differences must be kept in mind for effective administrative advocacy.

Let's consider the differences: Courts decide issues of individual or private rights. Part of the court's job is consider the public interest, but their express purpose is the *maintenance of the specific rights and privileges of individuals.* By contrast, administrative tribunals are established to *promote the public interest and implement policy decisions.* Of course, in performing this function, tribunals frequently impact on individual rights, but that effect is strictly collateral. This brings us to the first significant point: *In order to get a tribunal to act as you wish, you, the advocate, must couch the language of your submissions as that of public policy, not a private right.*

The policy implementation function of tribunals directly affects the choice of the people sitting on those tribunals. In the courts, judges are almost always lawyers. On tribunals, by contrast, the members are seldom lawyers. This means that the legal training a tribunal member has is often limited, and that brings us to point number two: *The tribunal's expertise as a whole is usually related (or limited) to the field in which the tribunal acts.*

WRITTEN ADVOCACY STANDS ALONE

In many cases, tribunals base their decisions solely on written materials, without the benefit of any oral argument or testimony. If that is how things work at the tribunal you're dealing with, considerable care needs to be given to ensure that your written materials say everything — there will be no opportunity to fill in gaps by oral argument. Many of the principles of drafting an affidavit for a motion or application apply equally to written evidence you prepare for a tribunal. Whether this evidence is going in by affidavit or otherwise, the evidence must be coherent and comprehensible. It must tell a story.

PREREQUISITES TO PREPARATION

Before preparing anything for submission to a tribunal, certain materials have to be obtained. At a minimum you must have:

1. The act and regulations governing the tribunal;
2. The rules followed by the tribunal; and
3. Previous decisions of the tribunal dealing with the issues raised by your client's circumstances.

It's also a good idea to get copies of previous applications and informational materials from the tribunal. After all, if you know how they made their decisions in the past, you'll have guidance on how to influence their decisions in the future.

Point number three is an obvious one, but it's still worth stating: *Tribunals are creatures of statute, and cannot do anything unless a statute or regulation allows them to do it.* Sorry if I've wasted your time in stating this, but it's amazing how often lawyers forget this point!

To apply this point, take a moment in your preparations to check the limits of the jurisdiction available to the tribunal before which you're appearing. Many tribunals have conditions precedent to the exercise of their jurisdiction; be sure you've met those conditions. Finally, somewhere in your written materials, it's a good idea to remind the tribunal where their jurisdiction is found to give you what you're seeking. Remember: Appointment to a tribunal is a classic political patronage plum — you may well find that you're making submissions to a member whose knowledge is peripheral at best. It doesn't have to be a big problem, though, provided you take steps to "lead him or her by the nose" down your path.

Here's something else to bear in mind: Tribunals exist to implement the policy decisions of the legislature. Accordingly, legislation that creates tribunals will usually be accompanied by some language setting out how the legislature expects the tribunal to act. The language granting and controlling the tribunal's jurisdiction is very important, and your attempts to influence the tribunal ought to use that same language. Don't be afraid to quote chapter and verse of a statute, and don't ever worry that the tribunal members have become bored hearing the same words used again and again by every advocate. On the contrary, it probably gives them comfort to hear those same words, and anyway, saying them is probably necessary to your submission. For example, if you do any criminal law, think of what you tell the judge when you're seeking a conditional discharge. If you don't rehash the relevant section of the *Criminal Code* for the umpteenth time, you're not doing your job.

Tribunals, in common with courts, tend to follow specific procedures in considering cases set before them. Where no special procedural code exists, they often follow some general legislative code which applies to all tribunals in that jurisdiction. Either way, it's a good idea to send a letter to the tribunal's secretary asking for the tribunal's rules or, if none exist, an outline of how the tribunal proceeds. A follow-up telephone conversation is often helpful. Remember, too, that you must ensure that the form your application takes is acceptable to the tribunal. If the tribunal uses standard form documents, these should be used; failure to use the tribunal's format can sometimes be interpreted as a lack of respect for the tribunal. Similarly, the standard forms ought to be completed in the customary form. Not only is this poor advocacy, but it starts you off with two strikes against you before you've uttered a word.

In common with the precedent used in civil litigation, it is helpful to get a precedent of the same type of filing you're going to make. The tribunal sometimes has information packages for this, and you should check to see if such helpful material is available. While written advocacy does require a creative approach, precedents of previous applications and tribunal information packets will tell you what the tribunal is looking for, and will allow you to tailor your documents to fulfil that need. Ask your friends, colleagues, bar admissions professors — somebody's bound to have a precedent. As an alternative, you can sometimes find previous applications at the tribunal itself, or in specialized libraries. But remember point number four: *Often, a tribunal is loath to decide an issue one way and then another -- such actions lack the appearance of justice. Nevertheless, tribunals do not follow precedent in the same fashion that courts do. Stare decisis* is not as absolute a principle in tribunals as it is in the courts. Sometimes, all you can expect from the past is a guide to the future. In this sense, previous decisions can be used as precedents. Read these previous decisions as part of your preparation, because the tribunal will often enunciate its policies there. These policies, together with the language used to describe these policies, will be used by the tribunal in all its decision making.

THE APPLICATION

Applications to tribunals usually are a combination of written argument and evidence. As such, applications to tribunals are different from documents you prepare for courts because the distinction between an application's evidence and argument is blurred. That said, except for matters that are widely known to everyone (for example, that it is generally cold in Ottawa during January), everything that you argue should be supported by evidence in some fashion. Moreover, that evidentiary support should be explicit, and easy enough to be seen even by the tribunal's patronage appointees. Even if tribunals lack legal training, they will implicitly ask the question "How do you know that is so?" whenever your application contains an assertion. The application itself must answer the question, simply because you will not be there in person.

The best format for an application (provided that it is not inconsistent with the rules of the tribunal) is similar to that of a factum used on a court motion, bound together with relevant evidence. Thus, the application has four basic sections:

1. Nature of application and jurisdiction;
2. Facts relied on;
3. Argument; and
4. Order sought.

The evidence bound together with the application doesn't always need to be in affidavit form. (Each tribunal has its own requirements.) But since affidavits are almost never forbidden, it's usually a good idea to put the evidence in sworn form.

NATURE OF APPLICATION AND JURISDICTION

As previously noted, tribunals are creatures of statute and cannot act unless they are authorized to do so by a statute or regulation. This is something important, so at the very outset of your application, you should tell the tribunal what the application is about and where the tribunal's authority to act arises. In most cases, jurisdiction is very clear, but even in such cases, it doesn't hurt to make explicit reference to authority. They may even be flattered that you have considered the extent of the tribunal's authority, and that will add credibility to the rest of your application.

This section need not be lengthy; a brief paragraph usually is enough. For example:

> *James Morton applies for a consideration of the Registrar's refusal to grant him a licence as a security guard at Havergal College. This tribunal is empowered to consider the Registrar's refusal, pursuant to [title and section of the regulatory authority] and, if it appears to be in the public interest, reverse such refusal and grant the licence.*

By reading a paragraph like the one above, the tribunal knows what the case is about and why the tribunal has the power to deal with it.

FACTS RELIED ON

Administrative matters seldom turn on novel legal issues. The facts drive the case and the determination will be based on the facts. Don't forget, however, that "public interest" and similar concepts are matters which may be considered relevant by the tribunal. This means that issues that are not relevant to most court proceedings (*e.g.*, the character of the applicant) can be relevant to a tribunal. Accordingly, the facts must be laid out in detail and everything which the tribunal considers important must be brought forward, which brings us to point number five: *In court-based factums, brevity is a great virtue; in the tribunal application, completeness is more important than brevity.*

Since the factual outline in an application is likely to be fairly lengthy, organization and format is important. Set out the facts in simple non-legal language and chronological order. Matters that are not chronological, say, issues relating to the applicant's character, are best to group at the end of the chronological outline. Subheadings are helpful and break up what might otherwise seem to be an overwhelmingly detailed factual recitation. Subheadings should be specific (*e.g.*, "Donald Breashear's Suitability for the Diplomatic Corps" and not "Character Issues") and fair (*e.g.*, "James Morton's Excellent Fitness as a Barkeeper" is not good).

You're trying to "sell" the tribunal on your idea, but be sure that the facts are set out in a way that at least appears to fair. Omit unhelpful facts and avoid misstating or omitting facts. You won't get away with it and, ultimately, it will weaken your application. State the facts fairly and use neutral language — to do otherwise insults the tribunal and weakens your case. (Think of how you felt when you first heard a portable tape player referred to as a "ghetto blaster", or a women's rights advocate called a "feminazi".) Remember: Your job is to persuade, not to offend.

Try to support your factual assertions the way you would in a factum. In fact, the physical appearance of this section resembles a factum. Each assertion is best followed by a reference to the page and line where the evidence may be found. If you're referring to a particularly pithy statement, a quotation of that statement is a good idea.

While the application may look like a factum, it shouldn't read like a factum. Legal language ought to be pared down to a minimum. Your language model in preparing an application should be that of a business memorandum.

ARGUMENT

The legal part of the argument ought to be kept to a minimum. The tribunal needs to know its jurisdiction in law, and your making a reference to earlier decisions may be helpful.[1] However, a detailed legal analysis will usually not help the tribunal, and may actually distract the tribunal from the analysis needed.

Policy arguments are usually more helpful to the tribunal. Set out the policy that the tribunal is trying to put into place and explain how granting the order you want promotes and fosters that policy. At the

---

[1] Attach any relevant statutes, regulations or prior decisions as schedules to the application.

very least, explain how granting the order sought does not hinder the tribunal's stated policy.

Recognize that tribunals, like all other regulatory bodies, often have unwritten rules. Sometimes a tribunal has jurisdiction to do something but it seldom or ever exercises that jurisdiction. Preparation, by discussion with the tribunal's secretariat or counsel who practise frequently in the area, will let you know if what you are seeking is highly unusual. If you are asking for something unusual, mention this early in your application, and explain why, in this situation, the unusual relief ought to be granted.

ORDER SOUGHT

Some care should be given to crafting the order you are seeking. In a civil court, it's considered proper to provide the judge with a draft order in your motion materials. If you're going to be in front of a tribunal, however, providing a draft order before a decision is rendered is often considered presumptuous and imprudent. Why the difference in attitude? Who knows. Just don't do it.

Sometimes a draft order can be prepared in advance, but be sure to keep it inside your briefcase until after you have been granted what you've asked for. Even then, unless it is urgent that something be on paper right away, it might be more prudent to let the tribunal take its time and draft up their own order. You may have to appear before that tribunal again in the future, and the last thing you want is to leave behind the impression that you're a smart-aleck who thinks he or she can read the future. If you absolutely have to give them a pre-drafted order, be sure to offer it to the tribunal with words like "Due to the nature of the crisis which has brought me before you today, which makes time of the essence, I have taken the liberty of drafting an order for your consideration. Please tell me if it is in any way deficient."

One further hint: In your draft order, be sure to make reference to the statutory or regulatory authority allowing the tribunal to act.

EVIDENCE

Not all tribunal applications require affidavit evidence. Sometimes it is proper to put correspondence or reports to a tribunal without affidavit support. If no affidavit is used, be sure to provide extra detail by including a documentary index. Tribunal members get upset when they have to wade through an unindexed (or worse, an unpaginated) document brief, which will certainly hurt your position. Regardless of how you structure it, ensure that the evidence before the tribunal is useable and easily accessible.

An affidavit is generally the proper way to support an application. This affidavit ought to tell a story and flesh out the facts not mentioned in other documents. To be most useful, the affidavit ought to follow the same format as the application itself.

The affidavit or other evidence ought to contain all the detail that is omitted from the text of the application. Remember: The tribunal will consider and be convinced by the factual outline in the application itself; the evidence should be there for the tribunal to refer to as necessary. For this reason, it does no harm to put excessive detail into the evidence. If the tribunal doesn't need it, they won't bother reading it. If they do need it, it's available.

The typical example of detail omitted in the body of the application but included in written evidence is a legal description of land. For the application, it's usually sufficient to describe a property as "the house municipally known as 24 Sussex Drive, Ottawa". In the evidence, you can include as an exhibit to an affidavit the title abstract, which can provide the tribunal with the legal description of this shack.

FOLLOWING UP ON THE APPLICATION

Once the application is filed, most tribunals will review it and ask for further materials or some amendments to the application. Obviously you will take such a request seriously and respond to it promptly and fully. If a particular request for information cannot be complied with immediately (say, because the response requires further investigation or review), tell the tribunal when it can expect your response, and make sure a response is delivered when promised. A failure to respond fully (or at all) will dramatically lessen the effect of the application, and may even lead to it not being proceeded with promptly or at all.

There is often some delay between the time an application is made and when a response of any sort is received from the tribunal. If the delay is lengthy (say, more than a couple of weeks), it is wise to write to confirm that the application was received and that everything is in order. Such a letter often ends up in the file with your application, and is likely read by the decision maker, so be sure not to seem presumptuous in asking whether everything is filed. If the tribunal feels that the applicant is trying to rush the decision or is disdainful of the tribunal, the applicant is not well served. Something along the following lines will do:

As you may recall, we act as counsel to [name of party] *and filed an application on behalf of* [name of party] *on* [date] *seeking* [remedy or order sought].

Since we have not heard anything from you since the filing we are concerned that perhaps we have not completed the steps necessary for you to consider the application. Is something still outstanding? The favour of reply in this regard would be greatly appreciated.

Yours respectfully,

[signature, etc.]

UPDATING OR AMENDING THE APPLICATION

As materials come in, or as situations develop, it sometimes becomes necessary to add to or amend an application. Provided you give proper notice, almost all tribunals permit the updating or amending of an application. Significant amendments, however, should not be made lightly, as they delay the application and, unless they are made in the face of significant and unexpected circumstances, weaken the application. Think of it this way: If you were comfortable with the initial form of the application, why did you change it? If you were not comfortable with the initial form, why did you file it?

If you plan to make significant changes, there's a danger that the application may become awkward to use. If you really want to annoy a tribunal, just ask them to look at several different document books and then realize, on reading earlier documents, that they've been wasting their time. It's hard to persuade an irritated tribunal, so avoid the irritant in the first place by preparing a fresh amended application. The tribunal's staff should be told what you're doing, so be sure to include a covering letter with your amended materials. In fact, this is one circumstance where you might be better off going into the tribunal office yourself and personally explaining to the registrar what is happening.

A FINAL WORD

Advocacy before a tribunal is precisely the kind of work where good legal writing will be rewarded. So find yourself a tribunal, locate a client who needs to apply to it, do your good legal writing, and reap your rewards.

Chapter 12

LETTERS, PART I

INTRODUCTION

Legal correspondence is a critical part of written advocacy. It's also the part you'll be doing most often. On any given day, a lawyer will send and receive a dozen of letters or more. How you produce and deal with letters will be a measure of your success in the practice of law.

Each letter you send or receive forms part of a running record of a legal matter. Think about the last time you were given carriage of a file which was already in progress. How did you bring yourself "up to speed" on it? Sure, you would have read the pleadings and motion records, but to really get the flavour of what the file was all about, you would want to read the correspondence file from start to finish. You can learn a lot from correspondence, not only about the case itself but also about the lawyers who are handling the litigation. Letters paint a vivid picture — real or otherwise — of their authors. Is the author precise or sloppy? Reasonable or a sabre-rattler? Is the other side's approach conciliatory, or is "J'accuse" the operating byword?

Carelessly drafted letters can lead to disaster. More generally, letters set the tone in an adversarial situation. Reasonable, professional and amicable correspondence leads to reasonable, professional and amicable settlements; the reverse is also often true.

KNOW YOUR AUDIENCE

When writing a letter, remember that at least two audiences may read it: The immediate recipient and a court. You can even add a third audience to the list: The Law Society or other professional regulating body for lawyers. If you send correspondence which is rude or unprofessional, you are definitely inviting the intervention of the complaints and discipline department.

This trinity of audience applies to all correspondence, including letters. Accordingly, a good rule to follow is to assume that every letter you write will some day be read aloud in court. If that thought makes you pause, then think carefully about sending the letter. Remember: When you write a letter, you are writing to the world.

INVISIBILITY

It is a maxim in legal practice that legal correspondence should be invisible. This is another way of saying that the reader of a legal letter should not notice the language of the letter itself, but should be able to immediately understand the meaning of the letter. Think of language as a lens through which meaning is perceived. Your goal is to create the impression of impassive but unmovable professionalism.

Think for a minute about the image of lawyer. In Canadian legal practice, the lawyer is an advocate, someone elevated from the dispute at hand, who takes no part in the emotions of the parties. Bearing this in mind, the preferred tone of a lawyer's correspondence should be somewhat distant, making it clear that the lawyer is not a party. Does this mean that you must sound unemotional? Certainly not. Affability, courtesy and concern are all emotional states, and they can contribute to the smooth resolution of the case. On the other hand, outrage, nastiness and bullying are unhelpful characteristics for a detached advocate.

Let's look at two lawyers' letters for the same scenario. Here are the facts: Your client owns a country property next door to a farm that raises horses. The client has come to you complaining that the horses' waste products have leached into the water table and have poisoned his well. You sit down and send off the following letter:

April 13, 2001

Edward Equus
Northern Dancer Side Road
Pegasus, Ontario
L0T 2G0

Dear Mr. Equus:
                    re: Disposal of Animal Waste

I am counsel for Anna and Frank Drinkwater.

As I am sure you are aware, Mr. and Mrs. Drinkwater have recently become concerned by your decision to store horse manure and other animal waste products close to the line which divides your property from theirs. As you also know, the Drinkwater family well is located only ten feet from the property line. Experiences ten years ago with the previous owner of your property have shown that biowaste stored this close inevitably leaches into the water table and thereby contaminates their well.

I need not recount to you the litigation which arose in 1991, eventually resulting in judgment against that owner.

The problem of biowaste storage is easy to resolve: All you need to do is to store it on the opposite side of your property. I am gratified to learn from my clients that this is what you have been doing of late. Please continue to do so. As well, would you kindly move the biowaste stored near the Drinkwater well to the other side of your property as soon as possible.

Please feel free to call me if you wish to discuss this further, or if I can be of any further assistance to you.

Yours very truly,

E. P. Taylor

A letter like this one is not guaranteed to bring the result you're seeking, but you've done everything right by wording it this way. If Mr. Equus continues to act like a bad neighbour, draft an injunction application for court and, as part of it, include this letter. Judges read correspondence between litigants closely, and you will be able to stand up in court and say "Your Honour, as you can see from the letter at Tab Q, we have done everything possible to resolve this dispute without wasting precious judicial resources. Sad to say, Mr. Equus has left us no choice". The judge will nod sagely and grant your injunction, with, let's hope, serious costs against Equus.

But what sort of costs would you expect at a future court appearance if you choose to send a letter that reads like the following?

April 13, 2001

Edward Equus
Northern Dancer Side Road
Pegasus, Ontario
L0T 2G0

Dear Mr. Equus:

re: Disposal of Animal Waste

I am counsel for Anna and Frank Drinkwater, a couple of neighbours whom you are obviously trying to poison.

Don't pretend that you are unaware that horse manure and other disgusting animal waste products are being stored close to the line which divides your property from theirs. If you had half a brain, you'd know that their well is located only ten feet from the property line. The previous owner of your property — another dipstick — had to be hauled into court in 1991, eventually resulting in judgment against him.

This is to put you on notice that you'd better store your biowaste on the opposite side of your property. My clients tell me that this is what you have been doing of late, and you'd better be damn sure you keep it up, or else. And please get off your fatty acids and move the biowaste already stored near the Drinkwater well as soon as possible. Otherwise, we'll see you in court.

Govern yourself accordingly.

Yours very truly,

E. P. Taylor

This example is exaggerated, of course, but you get the idea. Think of what a judge might do to you if the matter got to court and Mr. Equus asked her or him to read that second letter. The award of costs might well be as diminutive as your IQ for sending such an inflammatory letter in the first place.

Incidentally, did you notice that last paragraph, "Govern yourself accordingly"? GYA (as it's known) is a fairly provocative statement, and on the borderline of being considered rude. Use it sparingly and only for emphasis in situations where the goodwill between you and the other side is already at the zero mark.

HIM (OR HER) OR US?

There is a question whether letters ought to be framed individually or in the plural. More exactly, when you're writing about some step where you, the lawyer, will clearly be involved, should you talk about yourself ("me") or about the team of you and the client ("us")? Obviously, if the client is going to be participating personally (at a meeting, for example), you will use "we" and "us". But what if it's something that only you will be doing?

One school of thought says that, when the lawyer is part of a multi-lawyer firm, it is more appropriate for her or him to speak on behalf of the entire firm. In that case, "we" is the operative pronoun. For the sole practitioner, everything will be phrased in the singular. Opinions vary, but we recommend that, for members of a firm, the better choice is to write everything in the plural.[1] Writing in the plural adds distance between the lawyer and the situation and gives a more professional tone.

---

[1] As in "We have been consulted by you".

GENDER NEUTRALITY

Ask any family law lawyer: There is no such thing as gender neutrality.

In the context of legal writing, however, "gender neutrality" is a term for describing a writing style where the third person is not referred to as either male or female. Depending on your personal viewpoint, gender neutrality is either a reflection of reality, an expression of social concern, a courtesy to members of the underrepresented gender, or simply being polite.

The bad news about gender neutrality is that, at this point in the evolution of the English language, there is no easy way to achieve it. Your response to the situation may be to simply not care and stop worrying about the problem. But if gender neutrality is important to you, this is a list of ways it's currently being accomplished (more or less).

1. He or she (a.k.a. she or he). This one works because it covers both possibilities. Perhaps it would have sounded tautologous a decade ago if you wrote "Let us bring the matter before a judge of the bankruptcy court, and see what she or he will rule". Today it would sound quite normal, and indeed would reflect the reality that there are both female and male jurists sitting in most of our courts.

2. The plural "they". Grammarians long ago realized that the third person plural is gender neutral. It wasn't long before someone tried to use the word "they" as a singular pronoun. We can't say, at this writing, that the experiment is overwhelmingly entrenched in the language, but it is becoming more acceptable to write "Please take this document to your lawyer and see if they are satisfied with what it says".

3. Alternating "he" and "she". The principle behind this approach is a simple one: If you're going to be referring to a number of situations where the participants will be of both genders, simply say "he" one time and "she" the next time. It makes your writing sounds less awkward than it would be if you used the other methods, and no one will accuse you of sexism — as long as they're aware that you're using this convention. (Did we just use the singular "they"? Oh oh...)

Finally, there's this one, which is perhaps the best of the lot:

4. Do a tapdance in your writing to avoid situations where you have to be gender-specific. For example, don't write "Take your approved draft to the court clerk and have her sign it." Instead, write "Take your approved draft to the court for the signature of the clerk." Male clerks everywhere will thank you for your thoughtfulness.

By now, you will certainly be familiar with the accepted practice of avoiding a gender-specific label on a position or job. In this vein, "chairman" has become "chair", "alderman" has become "councillor", and "cleaning woman" has become "cleaner". The reason for this goes beyond political correctness; a good lawyer never wants to learn that she or he has given unintended insult to a correspondent. Many people take these matters quite seriously and personally. What is to be gained by annoying them, especially if you can avoid it?

FORMALITIES

A letter that is odd stands out and immediately loses credibility. While it may seem pedantic, don't forget that you never get a second chance to make a first impression. Therefore, sticking to the standard practices of letter-writing is essential if you want your correspondence to be taken seriously. Following, you will find a few of these formalities.

DATE LINE

Letters should be dated with the date of transcription, not the date they were dictated, unless there is good reason to do otherwise. There will be occasions when a letter becomes stale or overtaken by late-breaking events by the time it is typed. In such a case, it is perfectly proper to add a postscript, in hand, saying that the letter is being sent for confirmatory purposes. You should also outline briefly what the existing situation is. Don't make the mistake of writing a postscript as long as the letter it's appended to. If the postscript needs to be extensive, then the entire letter ought to be rewritten. The unsent letter may be kept for the file but marked "Unsent — events superseded letter".

SALUTATION

"Salutation" is the word for the "Dear [name]" beginning of the letter. The salutation you use is a matter of taste. You usually can't go wrong if your salutation reads "Dear [Mr. or Ms.] So-and-so". If your tastes run to the more stiff and formal, then write "Dear Sir" or "Dear Madame", as the case may be.

Your choices get more interesting when there is more than one recipient of a letter. In the old days, when a letter was addressed to a firm of lawyers, albeit to the attention of an individual,[2] the traditional salutation

---

[2]   As in a letter addressed:
    A, B and C
    Barristers and Solicitors
    Attention: C

was "Dear Sirs", regardless of the gender of the members of the firm.[3] Today, that sort of salutation would be considered sexist and inappropriate by many lawyers. If your recipients are all male, you can safely begin your letter with "Gentlemen". Unfortunately, if your recipients are all female, you may (or may not) get in trouble with the salutation "Ladies", as it could be perceived as patronizing. To avoid gender-specific language, try using the salutation "Dear Counsel". You can also fall back on an itemized listing, such as "Dear Mr. X, Ms. Y, and Dr. Z". Remember: Awkward beats insulting every time.

When writing to an individual known well to the writer, it is sometimes appropriate to strike, in hand, through the salutation and write a first name. Discretion should be used here, because you don't want to be perceived as being too chummy with the other side, either by your client or (far worse) by the recipient. (I was once reviewing a divorce file which had been transferred to me in mid-stream by an anxious client who thought his former counsel wasn't fighting hard enough for him. Imagine how the client and I felt when we saw that all correspondence from the other side's lawyer began with the salutation "Dear Bob"!)

When writing to judges or persons holding formal office, it is important to address the salutation by the title of the formal office.[4] The introductory "Dear [name]" is omitted in such cases, and replaced by "Your Honour", "Your Excellency", "Chief Justice", or whatever you might call this person in public.

SUBJECT LINE

The subject line of a letter is also known as the "re: line". The formal legal letter *always* contains a subject line. The subject line is usually a no-brainer; it identifies the case and, sometimes, the particular subject of the letter. Here's an example:

> *re:* ***Brashear v. McSorley***
> ***Request for Replacement of Broken Stick***

When listing the two litigants, it is conventional to put the name of the recipient's client first. Thus, in the example above, the letter was written by counsel for McSorley and sent to counsel for Brashear. Had it been the other way around, Brashear's counsel would have sent a letter to McSorley's lawyer with the "re: line" reading **re: McSorley *ats* Brashear**. The word *ats* is an acronym which stands for "at the suit of".

If litigation hasn't yet begun, you may wish to tone down the confrontational side of the subject line and write **re: McSorley and Brashear**. By using the word "and", you are subtly conveying the message "There

---

[3] The usage of "Dear Mesdames" for a firm of exclusively women lawyers, while proper, is archaic: E. Swartz, *Procedures for the Legal Secretary* 5th ed. (Toronto: Holt, Rineholt and Winston, 1993), p. 48.

[4] For example, "Registrar" or "Provost".

is no formal dispute presently in the legal system. Maybe we can work this out."

A word of caution: Subject lines are danger spots for the accidental disclosure of information. A subject line with a client's name and the general form of a litigation issue may disclose otherwise confidential information. Consider otherwise unexceptional requests for information, say from a financial institution, with the following subject lines:

re: James Morton, Impaired Driving Charge

or

re: James Morton, Mental Competency Hearing

or

re: James Morton, Matrimonial Claims

Any of these subject lines could lead to a withdrawal, or at least review, of bank credit. A neutral subject line, such as **Re: James Morton, Banking Information**, would serve the purpose just as well.

TEXT OF A LEGAL LETTER

Up to now, we have considered what should go into the structure of legal correspondence. In this section, we will consider the form of the text itself.

Except in extraordinary cases, letters ought to begin by stating why they are being written. Letters should also identify the writer, unless an ongoing correspondence makes this unnecessary, and the context of the writing. Here's a simple letter seeking to obtain Crown disclosure:

May 31, 2002

Crown Attorney's Office
attention: Disclosure Clerk
Ontario Court of Justice
123 D'Arcy McGee Avenue
Apsley, Ontario

To Whom It May Concern:

re: Morton, J.
Impaired Driving
Next Appearance
Date: _____

As you may know, we act as counsel to James Morton, who stands accused of impaired driving. We write for the third time (see attached) requesting disclosure.

This opening makes it very clear to the reader who the writer is and what it is they are seeking. Notice that the writer has also attached previous letters asking for the same thing. This practice is both a way of nagging the recipient, and also, by implication, conveying a subtle threat that there may be a motion down the road if the requested disclosure isn't produced soon. Remember: Each letter creates a record which can be shown at a future date to a judge.

All letters should close with a request that some step be taken. While this may seem repetitious, it is not a repetition to avoid. A senior lawyer once described the legal letter by saying "It begins by saying what I will ask for, it then says what I want, and closes by saying what I asked for". Let's look at the complete letter we examined a moment ago:

As you may know, we act as counsel to James Morton, who stands accused of impaired driving and we write for the third time (see attached) for disclosure.

We need disclosure to advise our client and prepare for a Crown pre-trial. In spite of three prior requests we still do not have it. Please send us the disclosure or call to let us know when it will be ready to pick up.

We do not wish to move in court for the disclosure but will be forced to do so unless we hear from you in the next ten days.

Your expeditious handling of this matter would be greatly appreciated.

This letter is very clear and serves as the basis for a motion. Nothing would be added by pointing out how inept they were for failing to provide disclosure by now. As the old saying goes, you can catch more flies with honey than you can with vinegar.

Footnotes and endnotes are rarely seen in legal letters. If you need to refer to a piece of case law, it is better to keep the citations in the body of the text.

Headings are commonly seen in letters, especially long letters. Headings will clarify and organize long letters, and also serve to calm a recipient who gets a five-pager and instinctively cries out "Omigod! I've got to read through all of this!" If you're going to use headings, your choice of language should not be haphazard. Keep it neutral, describing the content of the paragraphs to follow. Avoid vague headings such as "Legal Analysis", and instead write something like "Liability of an Employer for Acts of an Employee".

LEAD US NOT INTO TEMPTATION

Occasionally you will be tempted to write something theatrical in your legal letters. For example, let's say you represent a client who is in negotiations to sell shares of a company. Your client wants to get $3 a share. The solicitor representing the prospective buyer writes to you offering 12.5 cents per share. You are sorely tempted to respond to this absurd communication with the words "Are you nuts?" or "Your last offer is an insult and your mother is ugly, too!" — but this urge should be avoided. Such letters will make no sense except in the context of other correspondence, which may not be available later. Remember: A judge could potentially read your letter some day in the future!

This does not mean that dramatic expressions or theatrical responses to ridiculous letters ought to be avoided at all costs. Let's say they should be avoided only 99.9 per cent of the time. If the representative of the other party is your favourite sister, and she owes you a lot of money, and you have photographic evidence of her doing things that are unbecoming to a solicitor, then you can get away with outrageous content in a legal letter. Otherwise...

COMPLIMENTARY CLOSE

There are two aspects to the complimentary close: What close should be used and in what capacity the close is signed. Most legal letters are signed "Yours very truly". This is appropriate, except when you're writing to judicial or quasi-judicial officers, when the appropriate complimentary closing is "Yours respectfully" or just plain "Respectfully". The closing "Yours truly", while not wrong, is archaic and should be avoided.[5]

The capacity of signing depends, to some extent, on your personal taste. Generally, sole practitioners, or partners in law firms, should sign in their personal capacity:

Yours very truly,

_____

James C. Morton

Anyone else should sign as the law firm and not personally:

Yours very truly,

CALLINGBIRD, FRENCHHEN & TURTLEDOVE

Per: _____

    James C. Morton

---

[5] E. Swartz, *Procedures for the Legal Secretary*, 5th ed. (Toronto: Holt, Rinehart & Winston, 1993), p.51.

One final point: In most cases it makes very little difference if a letter is signed by a lawyer or for the lawyer by a secretary.[6] Correspondence ought not be delayed if a lawyer is out of the office when it is finalized and ready to go. There is one exception: All letters addressed to judges, or quasi-judicial officers, should be signed personally by the lawyer and not by a secretary.

COPIES

Standard legal practice is that letters copied to people other than the recipient are marked as being so copied.[7] You will always want to copy a letter to the client just to show them how you're right on top of the case. (It also protects you from a later accusation that you took steps without their knowledge or authorization.)

Some care should be used in copying letters, both from a tactical and from a legal standpoint. If a letter to counsel is, say, copied to the Law Society, the tone of the letter is significantly changed. Before copying a letter to anyone other than the client,[8] consider the impact of such copying on the tone of the letter.

With respect to legal implications, it must be remembered that if a letter to a client is copied to a third party, solicitor-client privilege may be impacted.[9] Further, the copying of correspondence can amount to publication for the purposes of defamation.[10] While you can argue that some qualified privilege may apply[11] in those circumstances, it is best to avoid the problem altogether.

The correct way to show that a letter has been copied is to write "c.c. [whomever]" after the secretarial attribution. Here's an example:

Yours very truly,
GRUMPY, SLEEPY & DOPEY

per: Snow White

SW/ab

c.c. Wicked Stepmother

---

6 As where a secretary signs for the lawyer:
    Yours very truly,

    Antman for JCM
    James C. Morton
7 Thus the comment at the end of a letter "cc: Client".
8 The client should always be copied on all correspondence.
9 *Wellman v. General Crane Industries Ltd.* (1986), 20 O.A.C. 384 (C.A.).
10 *Pullman v. Hill*, [1891] 1 Q.B. 524.
11 See, R. O'Sullivan, *Gatley on Libel and Slander*, 5th ed. (London: Sweet and Maxwell, 1960), Chapter B.

INFORMAL HANDWRITTEN NOTES

Not all letters sent by lawyers fall into the category of formal legal correspondence. Letters of congratulation or condolence are properly sent and are greatly appreciated. (Indeed, Hallmark has made a fortune on this very premise.) While such letters are generally informal, they do follow a standard form.

Unless written to very close friends, letters of congratulation or condolence should be sent on letterhead paper,[12] but *written by hand*. The subject line is omitted. The form of address and complimentary close remains as in formal letters although the addressee name is followed by a comma and not a colon (*e.g.*, a letter to a judge still begins, "Your Honour" and closes with "Yours respectfully"). The text is very short and omits the opening and closing, unless absolutely necessary. Finally, the first person singular is used throughout. A typical congratulatory letter might be as follows:

Your Honour,

I was delighted to learn of your recent victory in the Supreme Court Tiddleywinks Championship, and write to congratulate you. Kudos!

Yours respectfully,

In the next chapter, we will explore different types of legal letters, including solicitors' opinion letters.

---

[12] Some counsel have special letterhead paper for these letters that merely displays the counsel's name and business address, and omits the usual telephone, telecopier and electronic mail locators.

Chapter 13

LETTERS, PART II

INTRODUCTION

In the last chapter, we discussed lawyers' letters, the most common type of legal writing and, many would argue, the most important. Although the bulk of your lawyers' letters will be exchanged between counsel, other types of letters will come and go from your office, and it is important that you be familiar with how to write and respond to them.

Thus far we have considered the format of letters rather than their content. Let us now consider specific types of letters and what ought to be in each of them. No matter what type of letter you write, never lose sight of the theme of purposeful writing, and keep in mind that all letters may, eventually, be reviewed in court by a judge.

OPINION LETTERS

Two very different types of legal correspondence are both called opinion letters. The first type of opinion letter occurs in solicitors' work (as opposed to barristers' work). These opinion letters deal with issues such as title, security documents and ownership of property. Opinion letters of this type are very formal and follow a precise structure. This "boiler-plate" style technically removes such customary letters from the realm of written advocacy, but, for the sake of completeness, we will deal with them briefly. After discussing solicitors' opinion letters we will consider litigation, or barristers' opinion letters.

SOLICITORS' OPINION LETTERS

In virtually all significant commercial transactions, the investors or purchasers will require a favourable legal opinion dealing with such issues as legality of transaction, title, and any security interests created or existing in the property dealt with in the transaction. The purpose behind their getting the solicitor's opinion on paper is two-fold: First, the investors or purchasers want to be confident that they actually got what they paid for. Second, when a solicitor gives the client an opinion letter, she or he is putting a legal "seal of approval" on whatever is being discussed. Clients hire lawyers and pay them good money precisely to look out for their interests in a transaction, and they are within their rights to rely on the correctness of their lawyer's pronouncements when making their decisions. If some problem with the transaction arises later, guess what the aggrieved party can be expected to do? That's right — they will dust off their lawyer's opinion letter, plead the doctrine of detrimental reliance, and file suit against the lawyer who wrote it. Accordingly (as we lawyers say), it is essential that the opinion be prepared carefully and go no further than is absolutely necessary for the transaction.

The scope and contents of the opinion itself will normally be addressed to the client, who is usually an investor or purchaser. In a real estate transaction, the opinion generally comes from the lawyer acting for the purchaser; in other commercial transactions (say, a business refinancing), it is more normal for the opinion letter to come from the vendor or borrower's lawyer. In cases where the opinion is directed to someone other than the party for whom the lawyer giving the opinion has acted, it is common for the first draft of the opinion letter to be prepared by counsel for the party receiving the opinion letter. Believe it or not, it is often a material term of an investment or purchase that a satisfactory opinion letter be delivered and, accordingly, what is contained in the draft opinion letter can determine whether a transaction goes ahead or not.

The structure and scope of a solicitor's opinion letter depends on the nature of the transaction and the actual requirements of the parties. That said, the customary matters dealt with in an opinion letter generally include the following:

1. A brief description of the transaction.
2. A list of the documentation executed together with a list of the searches or investigations conducted by counsel and any assumptions relied upon by the lawyer giving the opinion.
3. A list of any documents registered and how such registration was made. Occasionally this section is merged with a section setting out the documentation executed. Such merger is not uncommon in small transactions, however, where a great deal of registration has occurred, details of such registration are usually broken out.
4. Details of any qualifications or limitations to the opinion. These qualifications can be very important since there are many things that counsel cannot have any personal knowledge of. For example, the solicitor giving the opinion will often have to rely upon certificates from corporate officers as to the factual underpinnings of the transaction. Similarly, counsel will not know if documents are what they purport to be or could, conceivably, be forgeries.
5. The actual opinion sought.

Legal opinions, just like any opinion you find in the rest of the world, cover an enormous range of topics. They can be as simple as commentary on a real estate transaction, indicating that a purchaser has obtained good title to a property. In business transactions, the opinions generally deal with matters such as the incorporation of a selling or borrowing company and its due organization and good standing. Other matters often dealt with include the power of the corporation to act; due authorization and execution of the transaction and a statement that the relevant agreements constitute valid, legal and binding obligations; the registration and ranking of security interests together with enforceability; and the capacity of the parties to enter into the transaction. (If reading the foregoing has you rolling your eyes, don't feel badly. Business law isn't for every lawyer — nor is making a good living!)

Most business or real estate opinion letters contain qualifications. In this case, the word "qualifications" does not refer to someone's training and experience. It refers to assumptions and presumptions, things which counsel expects are true. In the interest of safeguarding your exposure to a lawsuit, it is prudent to state you are assuming such things as documents being authentic, searches being valid as of the date of the transaction (even if only completed prior to the transaction closing), and that enforcement is subject to creditors' rights. Where currency other than Canadian is dealt with, it is customary to point out that Canadian courts can award judgment only in Canadian funds. Similarly, where foreign jurisdictions are involved, counsel ought to point out that they can opine only as to matters within the jurisdiction in which they practise, and opinions as to laws in other jurisdictions have to come from counsel qualified in those jurisdictions. When necessary and appropriate, reference can be made explicitly in the opinion letter to opinions from foreign counsel.

Any limitations or qualifications on the opinion ought to be clearly set out and tailored to the immediate transaction. Here are a few of the most common ones:

Authenticity

In giving this opinion we have assumed the authenticity of all documents submitted to us as originals and a conformity to original documents of all documents submitted to us as photostatic or certified copies. We have also assumed the genuineness of all signatures and that the signatures were made on or about the date or dates provided for in the documents there appended to.

Insolvency

The agreement constitutes a valid, binding and legal obligation of [party] enforceable in accordance with its terms except as enforcement may be limited by applicable insolvency, bankruptcy and other laws of general application limiting the enforceability of creditors' rights.

Jurisdiction

Our opinion is limited to matters governed by the laws of Canada and the Province of [name of province]. We express no opinion as to matters governed by laws of other jurisdictions and, specifically, in this regard, refer to the opinion of [name of solicitor] whom we have assumed to be a duly qualified member of the bar of [name of province]. We consider the opinion of [name of solicitor] as appropriate and rely upon it in granting the opinions given herein.

It should be noted that an opinion is always dated as of the date of closing and cannot opine on matters that will take place after closing.

Finally, unless you're a sole practitioner, you should remember that solicitors' opinion letters come from the law firm that employs you, and not just you as an individual lawyer. This means, of course, that if you've messed up, the firm will have to deal with the disgruntled client's negligence claim. In most firms, it is normal for solicitors' opinion letters to be signed by a partner. If an associate signs an opinion, it should be clear the signature is on behalf of the law firm and not the associate alone. (Most head hunters agree that attracting a major E & O claim for the firm is not considered a good way to advance toward partnership.)

LITIGATION OPINION LETTERS

The second type of opinion letter is found in litigation and is often known as a *litigation opinion* or a *barrister's opinion*. The purpose of the litigation opinion letter is to allow a client or potential client to decide whether to pursue or defend litigation. As such, *the language in the litigation letter must be appropriate to the client.* This means that, when you are writing to a new immigrant with poor English, the language should be simple, but not patronizing. By contrast, a letter on a civil contract breach to the in-house American attorney for a multi-national corporation should be written on a higher level.

Regardless of the level of language, the elements of the litigation opinion letter are fairly fixed. They are:

- The nature and scope of the opinion;
- Facts;
- Legal implications of the facts;
- Litigation avenues available;
- Costs of litigation and time frames;
- Chances of success; and
- Request for instruction.

Each of the elements of the litigation opinion letter forms a part of giving the client (or potential client) the ability to make an informed choice as to whether or not to pursue a case, or whether or not to pursue the case in a particular manner. Let's look at these elements one by one.

Nature and Scope of Opinion

This element outlines what the client has asked for and the limitations of the opinion. You should clearly state what question or questions the letter is intended to address and, just as important, what issues are not addressed.[1] Usually some reference to the uncertainty of litigation is appropriate; while all lawyers know that the best case is not a certainty, many clients do not know this, and the fact that any case may be won or lost should be mentioned. Here's an example:

> *You have asked us for an opinion of the legality of the transaction in the context of the laws of British Columbia as they existed on that date in 1966. You know, of course, that our office is situated in Halifax, and members of our firm are primarily conversant with the laws of Nova Scotia, not British Columbia. You should also recognize that the legal climate in 1966 was considerably different from what it is today, and this, too, would have had an effect on any case whose resolution was sought in the courts.*

Facts

It is essential to outline, in detail, the facts as they are understood by you, the lawyer, because these are the facts on which your opinion will be based. The client must be told that, if there are facts missing or if a court finds that other facts exist, the opinion's value falls dramatically. An appropriate beginning of this element might be:

> *We are basing this letter on the facts that follow. If we have misunderstood the facts, or if we have omitted anything you know of, let us know right away as that may change our opinion of your case. We are assuming that the facts that follow will be proven at trial and accepted by the court. If we cannot establish these facts, or if the court finds other facts to be the case, our opinion is going to be unlikely to apply.*

Legal Implication of Facts

It is important to discuss this element dispassionately, and to try to reflect both the legal points in favour of, and opposed to, your client's interests. While you should say what is the better legal position, a falsely dogmatic view does not give the client the ability to weigh options.

The level of detail provided in the legal review of the assumed facts depends on the client. For the less sophisticated client a review of basic concepts — including the structure of the court system and rights of appeal — is essential. Particularly for less sophisticated clients, a brief description of the likely steps in litigation (pleadings, motions, discovery, *etc.*) is helpful.

---

[1] For example, "You have asked us about the chances of voiding a transfer of property from your debtor to their spouse; in our analysis we have not considered bankruptcy or insolvency issues and have confined our review to provincial conveyance legislation".

The more sophisticated client, say an insurer, doesn't need to be reminded of such things as the fact that civil trials can be heard by juries. In letters to a sophisticated client, it may be appropriate to give case citations and even, on occasion, to attach case law. The detail of the legal review is a matter of discretion. Always remember that your goal is to place the relevant law before the clients and ensure that they understand it.

Here is an example taken from a child protection case, where the client is a rather unsophisticated woman whose children have been apprehended by the Children's Aid Society. She knows she is angry at what has been happening, and that's about all she knows. This opinion letter has the dual purpose of enlightening the client and also protecting the solicitor's position by making it impossible for her to later claim that her lawyer was keeping her in the dark.

You are well aware that the pivotal issue of this case is your mental health. The children were originally apprehended precisely because Children's Aid had concerns for your mental health and its alleged effects on the children. You told me that you found the Family Court Assessment Clinic to be heavy-handed and unreliable in making impartial evaluations of your psychiatric condition. (Having dealt with them myself, I largely concur.) We therefore took a great deal of time to find precisely the right psychiatrist — one well outside of the influence of the area of your home town — and had him make the evaluation. You may not agree with Dr. Jones's assessment of you, but you cannot deny that he has impeccable credentials and is totally impartial. I would suggest, therefore, that whether or not Dr. Jones's assessment is correct, we are stuck with it, and must proceed on the basis that it is accurate.

Throughout the case, you have always made a point of reminding me that your family law troubles go beyond the simple issues of mental health. You have asked me more than once to represent you in proceedings against the federal Government, the provincial government, and various police forces. I have told you on each occasion that I am only being paid by Legal Aid to represent you in the protection case brought by the Children's Aid Society. Without wishing to make an evaluation of the merits of your other cases, I will nevertheless say to you that you will bear a very heavy burden of proof if you are to succeed in any of your proposed litigations, and I doubt that you will get Legal Aid to fund them.

You have also indicated that you wish to sue the various agencies associated with your child protection case. These include, I believe, the Children's Aid Society, various foster parents, and the Family Court Assessment Clinic. As I have told you on more than one occasion, such litigation can only be commenced after the children are returned to your care and custody. Without meaning to sound paranoid, I suggest that if you try to sue them while they still have control over your children, you will simply be providing them with a greater motivation to find you mentally ill and unsuited to care for the children. As your trial must take place within the next year, a ruling one way or the other is bound to come down in the near future. I would therefore suggest that you be patient a little longer and hope that the children come back to you. Then talk about suing.

Litigation Avenues Available

This element is largely self-explanatory. The client needs to know what options are available. Often, the options are very limited, although in other cases numerous avenues for relief do exist. Regardless, the legally available options must be outlined and their respective advantages and disadvantageous explained. Practical issues should not be omitted. If, for instance, a family law client can seek relief in either the lower court or the higher court, you will want to mention such factors as the tendency of provincial judges to minimize support, or to award joint custody more freely than superior court judges.

Remember: Informed clients make informed decisions and are less likely to accuse you of professional negligence (or to succeed if they do).

Costs of Litigation and Time Frames

Clients are, understandably, anxious to know precisely what litigation will cost and when it will be completed. Unfortunately, these are two pieces of information which are frequently impossible to pin down. (Naturally, the client will think that you are a money-grubbing lawyer who is out to take the silver fillings from their teeth.) You can minimize this paranoia and gain credibility if you draft an opinion letter to the client that contains clear cost estimates and a hoped-for time frame for completing the case. Litigation is extraordinarily costly and slow; unless the client can accept this, it is better not to litigate.

Chances of Success

Clients will also want to know "Will I win?" Can you guarantee a victory in court? Of course not. Therefore, while a client is entitled to your professional view of the *likely* result of litigation, you must always make it clear that the best case can be lost, and the worst case can be won, all depending on matters wholly outside of counsel's control.

Here are two examples, one from a case with good prospects, and another from a case with poor chances of success.

> *Boris Badguy was noted in default in the civil lawsuit back in June. This means that he can no longer file a defence to your cross-claim, and it is now up to you to bring the matter to trial, if that is what you wish. As we both know, Badguy is most unlikely to contest this matter at all. Even if he knew about a motion for judgment, it is exceedingly unlikely he would bother to show up to make representations to the court. It is therefore open to you to go before the court with your default, provide some evidence of Badguy's fraud, and (in all likelihood) get judgment against him. This exercise would cost you perhaps $500, and would probably yield you nothing more than a piece of paper you could frame on your wall. Nevertheless, if this is what you would like to do, I will be happy to oblige you.*

> *At the present time, we are still waiting for a response from the defendants to the settlement proposal we put forward on September 17. I know that you are*

impatient to collect on the judgment which you obtained back in the spring. As I was explaining to your colleague, Ms. Sharmani, it is in our best interests to wait a little bit longer before we take any further steps. As you are aware, small claims courts are usually a lot more liberal about granting indulgences to parties who breech procedural rules. While a higher court would not be so willing to set aside default judgment, small claims court probably would, especially if the reason for the default was an error by the law student in the defendant's lawyer's office. On the other hand, we can likely mount an effective opposition to a motion to set aside the default judgment if a reasonably long period of time elapses and no action is forthcoming from the defendants. At that point, we can argue to the court that, if the defendants' were really sincere about wanting to defend, they would have taken expeditious steps as soon as they learned of the default judgment.

Request for Instruction

This element is not a pitch for business. The request for instruction is to protect you from later claims by a client, who took no steps to retain you, that the client thought you had proceeded with the action. A typical request for instruction is brief and might be written thusly:

We would be delighted to assist you in this matter if you choose to retain us. Unless we hear from you we will not take any further steps in this matter. Since, absent further instruction, our work is now complete, we will forward our account under separate cover. Thank you for consulting our firm.

Such a request for instruction is polite and seeks the client's retainer, but it also is clear that without the retainer, the lawyer will not pursue litigation.

REPORTING LETTERS

Closely related in purpose to the litigation opinion letter is the reporting letter. The reporting letter is designed to keep the client apprised of the course of litigation, as well as to give options for future direction and to ask for instruction. In effect, a reporting letter is a litigation opinion letter written during the course of litigation.

Reporting letters are as brief or as lengthy as the event they are talking about. When a fairly minor event in litigation has happened, a very brief reporting letter may well be all you need. The following example is a sufficient letter to report on receipt of a motion record to compel production.

As you know, the plaintiff has brought a motion to compel us to disclose your tax returns for the last three years. We refused this production during discovery because we believe the tax returns are irrelevant. That said, if we oppose the motion it will likely cost at least $[amount], and we may lose, in which case costs will increase. In our view, even though the tax returns are not really relevant, little turns on their production and it probably makes sense to *avoid the motion costs and produce the tax returns. Please let us know how you want to proceed.*

Of course, following a major step in the litigation process — say, an examination for discovery — a much fuller report is necessary. The key idea to keep in mind is the need to give the client enough information to make a sensible, informed choice as to what should be the next step.

"WITHOUT PREJUDICE" LETTERS

Many letters coming from lawyers, or others, have the phrase *without prejudice* written in bold, often capitals, somewhere on the letter. The phrase *without prejudice* is often misused and is widely misunderstood. As a general rule, letters written for the purpose of settlement of a dispute which are not explicitly made *with prejudice*, are privileged and not producible in evidence.[2] Thus, in *York (County) v. Toronto Gravel Road & Concrete Co.*,[3] the court notes:

> [O]vertures of pacification, and any other offers or propositions between litigating parties, expressly or impliedly made without prejudice, are excluded on grounds of public policy.

What this means is that marking a letter *without prejudice* is almost always meaningless. If the letter is for settlement of a dispute it is, automatically, without prejudice and admissions made in the letter are irrelevant and inadmissible.[4] On the other hand, if a letter is not for the settlement of a dispute, it is producible, if otherwise relevant and material, regardless of being marked *without prejudice*.

All that said, the marking of a letter *with prejudice* can be of considerable advantage. Such letters are producible during the course of litigation and, particularly if they show an intention to fulfil a legal obligation, can be very useful. Finally, because marking a letter *with prejudice* is highly unusual, such letters are usually read quite carefully.

LETTERS AS FORMAL STATEMENTS

Many statutes come with very specific forms, the use of which is enforced by fanatical court clerks and, every now and then, by the judiciary. Occasionally, however, a letter can serve in place of another formal

---

[2] See J. Sopinka, S. Lederman, A. Bryant, *The Law of Evidence in Canada*, 2nd ed. (Toronto: Butterworths, 1999), p. 720. Once the litigation is over, the letter is likely admissible regarding costs.

[3] (1882), 3 O.R. 584 at 593-94 (Ch. Div.); aff'd (1885), 11 O.A.R. 765 (C.A.); aff'd (1885), 12 S.C.R. 517.

[4] See *Derco Industries Ltd. v. A.R. Grimwood Ltd.* (1984), 57 B.C.L.R. 395 at 139-140 (C.A.).

legal document. Demands for particulars, for example, are usually made by letter rather than formally. In order to serve as a replacement for a more formal document, a letter must specifically state that this is its role. The way to do this is simply to use a sentence like "Please consider this [an offer to settle/a demand for particulars/*etc.*] under the Rules."

You can't use a letter to substitute for documents like a statement of claim, an affidavit, or many other things covered by the procedural rules of your jurisdiction. Before you send your letter, be sure it will be able to do the job you're asking of it.

DEALING WITH THREATENING LETTERS

In a perfect legal world, barristers and solicitors would all be upstanding members of the Bar who behaved like ladies or gentlemen (your choice). The unfortunate reality, however, is that it is almost commonplace to receive threatening letters from lawyers. As a class act, *you* would never send such letters, except in extraordinary circumstances. Nevertheless, when you receive such letters, they must be dealt with.

Rule number one when responding to threatening letters is to remember that anything a lawyer writes may end up being read by a judge. As a rule, judges don't like to see lawyers asking each other to step outside. Their reaction when they see such a letter will range from annoyance (at best) to seething anger. Here it is best to apply the same strategy you used as a child when your big brother hit you: Don't retaliate in kind; instead make sure that "mommy" is in a position to find out about the misdeed and get mad at the other person, not you.

The best response to a threatening letter is often to ignore the threat and deal with the matter about which the threatener is complaining. Take a moment to decide if the complaint might be legitimate. It's not unheard of for a well-meaning solicitor (even one as perfect as you) to inadvertently cause difficulties for another counsel, or even to inadvertently insult that counsel. If you realize you did do something incorrect, figure out how to fix it and convey your apologies to the rude correspondent. In passing, you might mention that your counterpart's reaction was, shall we say, a little bit choleric.

Let's suppose that you have not done anything wrong. Quickly review for yourself why your actions (or your style in performing them) were justified. When you reply to the threatening letter, be temperate and deal, at the outset, with the complaint raised. If it is without merit, say so and explain why. If the complaint is justified, agree and explain how you will fix the problem. Having dealt with the complaint, turn to the threat. The threat should be acknowledged and the fact of the bullying adverted to. That done, toss in a clear statement that no intentional wrongdoing was intended or occurred. If the threatener has said that she or he is going to bring your conduct to the attention of the court or the Law Society (or even the police), you may want to conclude your letter with a statement that a review of your conduct is welcomed. Such a conclusion almost always ends the threats.

Here is a sample response to a letter threatening a complaint to the Law Society for some imagined wrong:

We have in hand your letter of [date] *and write in reply thereto.*

With respect to the allegation that we improperly dealt directly with your client, we remind you of the provisions of [statute] *which requires* [steps taken].

In terms of your threat to report us to the Law Society, we respectfully take the position that this threat is quite improper and, indeed, is a breach of professional etiquette. We will not trouble ourselves further with your improper conduct. With respect to our conduct, you are welcome to report it to the Law Society and we welcome, as always, their review.

If you want to be a bit nasty, you can add this sentence:

For your convenience, the Law Society's address and telephone number follow:

[Address and telephone number]

Before leaving this topic, let us raise a caveat about frankly admitted error. If the error you've committed is small (say, putting a privileged document into a motion record by oversight), admit your mistake. If, however, the error is such that it could lead to possible personal liability (say, allowing the time to appeal a sentence to expire), make no admission without contacting your professional insurer and following the appropriate rules of professional conduct. Negligence (even the innocent or inadvertent type) is serious business for a lawyer. It's time to get your money's worth out of that E & O insurance you've been paying.

WRITING FIRM — NOT THREATENING — LETTERS

So much for what you should do if you receive a threatening letter. How about if you want to send one yourself?

The correct response to the question "Should I send a threatening letter?" is *no*. When you're writing to complain about the conduct of another lawyer (or her or his client), you can and should lay out options about what you might want to do. But never threaten. You'll achieve better results if you state facts, and do so politely and without rancour.

By the way, it is not a threat to write that, if a potential defendant doesn't make payment or do something else by a deadline date, you have instructions to commence a lawsuit. Similarly, it is perfectly proper to point out that, should a course of action be followed, personal liability to the solicitor may follow. Indeed, in some circumstances, such notification is a condition precedent to establishing the liability.[5]

Any letter asserting personal liability should be written with a tone more of sadness than anger, because — you guessed it — a court may well read the letter. An appropriate paragraph raising the issue of personal liability might be as follows:

> *We also must raise another, rather difficult, issue. Based on [rule or case] it appears that your office is directly and personally liable for [action]. We must ask you to take notice that our client will claim against your firm directly and personally.*

If you're going to introduce an element of anger into your letter, make it controlled anger. Be sure to refer to specific conduct you find unprofessional or offensive and, if possible, cite a portion of the statute or the Rules of Professional Conduct that you feel is being breached. Take a look at this example:

> *Further to our meeting in chambers last week, please find enclosed herein our* **Statement of Defence and Counterclaim**, *which we are serving upon you pursuant to the Rules.*
>
> *On a professional side note, I am going to renew the request I made to you after our meeting in chambers, namely that you kindly desist from making personal remarks of the sort that you did to His Honour. To be accused of perpetrating "shenanigans" on the court (to use your terminology) may not be a serious matter to you, but I do take it as a direct accusation of professional impropriety, and I do not appreciate your making such a statement about me to a judicial officer. I refer you to Rule 14 of the Rules of Professional Conduct, and specifically to paragraph 8 of the Professional Conduct Handbook, which states that lawyers "should avoid ill-considered or uninformed criticism of the competence, [or] conduct...of other lawyers."*
>
> *On the day in question, you responded to my request by stating that you were "just doing [your] job". It is apparent that your firm and mine have different perceptions of our jobs.*

RESPONDING TO COMPLAINTS FROM CLIENTS

As we discussed earlier, letters to clients are of great importance. Sometimes, as with opinion and reporting letters, considerable length and formality is necessary. Otherwise, a brief note keeping the client apprised is all that is needed. Regardless, the key is to keep the client informed and up to date in the litigation.

Most cases follow a pattern: Civil cases generally have discovery, settlement offers, pre-trials, *etc.*, while criminal cases have Crown

---

[5]   *Fekete v. 415585 Ontario Ltd.* (1988), 64 O.R. (2d) 542 (H.C.J.).

disclosure, plea negotiations, judicial pre-trials, and the like. A good practice is to write a standard letter that can be sent to clients at different stages. For civil clients, a good time to write such a letter is at the time of discovery; for criminal clients, you should write just after a Crown pre-trial. These letters deal with the general concerns the client will likely have, and many good sources for precedents exist.[6]

It is essential, even with good precedents, to review each letter before it goes to the client to ensure that it reflects the facts of the case. Care should also be taken to ensure that precedent letters are gender neutral, or, if they are not, that they be amended to reflect the gender of the client. It is profoundly embarrassing to have a client telephone and point out that they are a sex other than the one referred to in your last letter. (And even more embarrassing if the client makes suggestions about how to take advantage of such a situation....)

A difficult type of client letter is one that responds to a client's, often cruelly stated, complaints about your conduct. You'll get complaints a lot in your practice of law, and you've got to develop a thick skin when you receive them. Remember, client complaints often reflect their frustration at the situation and their inability to make it go away. Have compassion in these situations. Rather than responding in haste, put the complaint aside overnight and respond to it the next day and in writing.

Your responding letter should outline the client's concerns and address them one by one. Do not attack the client: Just respond to the concerns. It is best to point out that other counsel are available if the client has lost faith in you. Nineteen times out of 20, they will recoil in horror at such a suggestion.

Here is a complaint letter which a solicitor may receive, and a possible response to it:

Client's Complaint

You totally screwed up the last motion! You sent a student who didn't know what she was doing and you didn't follow any instructions to get an adjournment. Your excuses don't interest me — you are paid far too much and never even pay attention to what I say.

Solicitor's Response

We have your letter of yesterday's date and thought, in light of the serious issues it raised, we should respond in written form.

We did seek, as you requested, a further adjournment of the motion to [motion]. Our student, [name], was well versed in the case and the law and pointed out to the Master that we had just been retained. You may recall we agreed to send our student to save money on the motion.

---

[6] Manes, R., *Organized Advocacy* (Toronto: Carswell, 1983); Wunder, M. *Conduct of a Personal Injury Action* (Toronto: Carswell, 1970).

All that said, the Master refused a further adjournment and ruled against you. That result is disappointing, but it is a fairly small matter in the context of the case as a whole.

We are sorry you feel we have not responded to you as quickly as we ought to have. Obviously, we are busy but we do generally get back to you within a few hours of any telephone message.

Finally, we appreciate your business and want you to stay a client. Nevertheless, it may be you feel you can be better served elsewhere — if so we will be happy to assist your new counsel.

I will call you later today.

Naturally, having put that last sentence into your response letter, you should call the client and try to put the outburst behind both of you.

A FINAL WORD

The topic of legal letters is a vast one, and could legitimately be the subject of an entire book. We hope this has given you a good introduction to this area, and remember: Letter-writing is a skill that gets better with practice. Don't worry, you'll get lots of it!

Index